Great River Road

For Shelly,
In loving
friendship,
Mimi

Great River Road

MEMOIR and MEMORY

by Madelon Sprengnether

n
e
w
RIVERS
PRESS
MSUM

First Edition
Library of Congress Control Number: 2013950955
ISBN: 978-0-89823-312-4
e-ISBN: 978-0-89823-313-1

Cover design by Brittany Krebs
Interior design by Nayt Rundquist
Author photo by Michael Young

The publication of *Great River Road: Memoir and Memory* is made possible by the generous support of Minnesota State University Moorhead, The McKnight Foundation, the Dawson Family Endowment, the Lake Region Arts Council, Northern Lights Library Network, and other contributors to New Rivers Press.

   This publication is funded in part by a grant from the Lake Region Arts Council through a Minnesota State Legislative appropriation.

For copyright permission, please contact Frederick T. Courtright at 570-839-7477 or permdude@eclipse.net.

New Rivers Press is a nonprofit literary press associated with Minnesota State University Moorhead.

Alan Davis, Co-Director and Senior Editor
Suzzanne Kelley, Co-Director and Managing Editor
Wayne Gudmundson, Consultant
Allen Sheets, Art Director
Thom Tammaro, Poetry Editor
Kevin Carollo, MVP Poetry Coordinator
Vincent Reusch, MVP Prose Coordinator
Richard D. Natale, Production Consultant
Nayt Rundquist, Production Assistant
Val Oswald, Public Relations Assistant

Publishing Interns: Kjersti Maday, Lana Syltie

Great River Road: Memoir and Memory Book Team:
Jean Hellner, Karisa Kretschmer, Richard D. Natale, Erin Stegman

Printed in the USA
Great River Road: Memoir and Memory is distributed nationally by Small Press Distribution.

 New Rivers Press
c/o MSUM
1104 7th Avenue South
Moorhead, MN 56563
www.newriverspress.com

for Michael

Contents

Memoir and Memory, a Preface

It's a poor sort of memory that only works backwards.
—Lewis Carroll, *Through the Looking Glass*

In 2002, I turned sixty, my daughter married, and I published a memoir titled *Crying at the Movies*. At the time, this seemed like a remarkable concurrence of events—a series of life changes that must be significantly related. But how?

I'm not obsessive about birthdays, but sixty seemed like a milestone, signaling the passage from middle age into what? Old age? Late middle age? As the demographics of aging shift, so do the categories and the lines of demarcation between them.

For my grandmother's generation, sixty was old. With the exception of my paternal grandmother, who lived to be nearly one hundred, all of my grandparents died before the age of seventy. In their sixties, they saw themselves as elderly, and they looked it—silver-haired, somewhat bent, slow-moving, arthritic. But the average life span in the United States has increased dramatically over the course of the twentieth century—from approximately forty-eight at the beginning to nearly seventy-five by its end. My own mother died at age eighty-two and would have lived even longer if she'd attended more carefully to her health in her middle years.

My father's tragic death at age forty-two was the subject of my memoir, *Crying at the Movies*, in which I explored how feelings of unresolved mourning invaded and disrupted my adult life. Yet, because my dad died so young, he offered me no model—either positive or negative—of aging. If anything, I found myself surprised at having so dramatically outlived him. At sixty, I felt more like his mother than his daughter. What could he have told me, had he lived, that I didn't already know?

All of this is to say that I was radically unprepared to think about aging, yet I was now entering the territory that I had once defined as old. I consoled myself with the thought that I was not in fact yet old, as my life could well extend into my nineties. Who knows, I might even make it to one hundred! I thought of my dad's mother, hoping I'd inherited her genes.

More importantly, I had not thought about the difference between being (or feeling) solidly middle-aged and something else. How was this time of my life different from what had gone before? No matter that everyone said I looked younger than my years. I didn't feel bad about how I looked—at least not yet—the real issue for me was that I didn't know how I felt within. This territory was uncharted. I was beginning a journey that was unlike any other—a journey that had only one destination, no matter how distant or deferred: death.

I'd already survived longer than most people would have at another time or in another (less privileged) part of the world. I'd had rheumatic fever as a child—three times with increasing severity, at a time when penicillin was just beginning to be prescribed for ordinary use—and had two different types of cancer in my adult life, fortunately both curable. Throughout these various ordeals, I had good health care and excellent doctors, who, in effect, saved my life.

It wasn't as if I was unaware of mortality. Rather, I was just beginning to appreciate my extraordinary good luck in having come so far. But sheer relief was not enough. At sixty, I'd already lived more of my life than I had left to live, which meant that my life was as much grounded in memory as in present or future action. With each forward glance, I was also looking back. If anything, past and present now seemed commingled to the extent that I could no longer separate them. Experience in the moment embraced both in ways that also began to affect my anticipation of the future.

How to give words to such an elusive awareness? Especially now that memory itself is so much in doubt—less a certifiable entity than a mirage or fleeing shadow.

Cognitive neuroscience offers a guide through this phantom world. Personal memory, it tells us, is an absent presence—something that happens, brain-wise, in the moment, but refers to feelings or events that occurred in another time and place. The very process of remembering is fluid and volatile, dependent as it is on the activation of neural pathways in the brain, at the same time that it occurs in response to an absent experience or awareness.

Though it refers to something past, memory can only happen in the present. A neuro-chemical—yet also unreal—reality. You cannot take hold of memory. You can only comprehend it as paradox.

My daughter's wedding, in the early summer of 2002, foregrounded these issues. It was here that I began to think about my age, my past, and my experience in the present differently.

I had been used to thinking of the past as traumatic, something I'd labored to overcome or forget. *Crying at the Movies* explored this reaction and its painful consequences for much of my adult life. Not having mourned my father when he died, I found myself re-experiencing his loss in a variety of displaced ways in my middle years. Concluding *Great*

3

River Road felt like a relief, but I did not anticipate any radical change in myself or the way that I lived. It was enough, I thought, to have said what I needed to say.

Yet, the very act of having defined the parameters of my childhood loss subtly altered them. Suddenly, my past was accessible to me in a new way—no longer as something to avoid or suppress, but as a field of resonance.

At my daughter's wedding, I sensed this shift without having a language to describe it. Instead, what I felt was a kind of happiness I'd not experienced since I was a child. I was, for a brief though memorable period of time, euphoric. Yet, I was also immersed in, and suffused by, memory. My pleasure in the moment was underpinned and enriched by the density of my reminiscences. It was as if I lived simultaneously in the present and the past, neither vying with the other, but rather each contributing to something vibrantly new.

Although the euphoria faded, the feeling of inner change did not. Somehow, without conscious effort, my life had taken an unexpected turn. It was as if I'd been released from tragedy into a lighter, more comic mode—as in one of Shakespeare's late plays, where storm and shipwreck lead not to death and destruction but to reconciliation and transformation.

Lines from Shakespeare's *The Tempest* came to mind—where Ariel sings to comfort Ferdinand, who believes his father drowned.

> Full fathom five thy father lies;
>   Of his bones are coral made;
> Those are pearls that were his eyes:
>   Nothing of him that doth fade
> But doth suffer a sea-change
> Into something rich and strange.

When I first encountered this play, I took these lines personally. Drowning was *my* father's fate. Yet, I could not picture anything beautiful emerging from such a terrible story. Now I began to reconsider.

My father's body would never turn into anything other than what it was: his decomposing remains. But perhaps his lifeline, as represented in me, might have another trajectory? And what about memory, so seemingly fixed, yet also so flirty, so malleable?

At the root of the word memory—which gives rise to such words as commemorate, memorial, and memoir—lies the Latin *memor*, meaning to be mindful. Also the Old English *murnan*, meaning to remember sorrowfully, or to grieve. Mindfulness and mourning. Another conundrum.

To be mindful—that is to say fully present in the moment (to borrow the language of mindfulness meditation)—may also include remembering, which is to say being aware of what is not present, hence open to loss. Conversely, to remember is to re-member, to reconstruct or recreate, thus generating a new state of consciousness. Not only can you simultaneously inhabit the seemingly fixed past and the fluidly volatile present, but by that very act of mind you may alter both.

When I began writing *Great River Road*, I had something like a vision, not the transcendent kind where you are taken out of yourself and rapt into another world, but rather something like a shift of focus or attention—so mundane that it seemed at first more like an idea than a vision, yet so marvelous that it also felt like a revelation.

This vision had to do with memory and with a change in relation to my past that I began to experience as a result of writing *Crying at the Movies*. It came to me as a feeling of euphoria in the summer of 2002. It seems important to me now that this vision came to me in the form of happiness—as a feeling of supreme well-being coupled with a sense that my entire history was enfolded in the present moment. So powerful was this feeling that I even had a fleeting sense of destiny, as if all the scattered and seemingly unrelated parts of my life had conspired to lead me to this one encompassing awareness.

This happiness did not last, but it left me with an image of what I had felt—along with a perception of how different it was from anything I'd ever known. Because it was so hard for me to describe or hold on to, I began to use a shorthand term for it: pleroma.

I'm not sure when I first encountered this word—Greek in origin, referring to fullness or completion and later Christianized to mean the fullness of the presence of God—but it appealed to me immediately. I thought of pleroma then (and now) as something like the reunion of the blessed in heaven. I thought of it as paradise, but not the kind that separates the worthy from the unworthy, rather the kind of paradise that the painter Sir Stanley Spencer might imagine—where everything lost (good, bad, or indifferent) is restored. I liked this idea so much that I savored it in my imagination, despite the fact that I'd long ago given up my childhood belief in life after death.

When I had my private vision in the summer of 2002 at my daughter's wedding, it had everything to do with memory and nothing, it seemed, to do with heaven. Yet, the sense of completion or fullness of being that I experienced as the result of the convergence of past and present in that moment felt resonant with the idea of pleroma—a state of gratification associated with an unearthly feeling of benediction. This, I thought, is what memory made present and manifest can accomplish.

This train of thought was in tune with what I was discovering from the new neuroscience, which reminds us of the obvious—that experiencing a memory can only happen in the present and, as such, is a part of present awareness, suffusing, expanding, and interacting with it in unpredictable ways. What we "remember" is thus happening—and forever changing—in the present.

Our language for this process is awkward and unwieldy. We use nouns—past, present, memory—which imply separate and static conditions, rather than the active, volatile, and fluid engagement that actually occurs. If we must use a part

of speech for memory, it should be a verb instead of a noun—
something that includes the connotations of musing or reminiscing. When Marcel Proust titled his monumental reverie
on time past, he chose the phrase *à la recherche*, meaning that
he was seeking something, so that his whole long novel, *In
Search of Lost Time*, constitutes a quest, emphasizing the process of going forth, over arrival.

I've often thought of writing as a means of moving forward—
in an almost literal way, like walking across a field—but never
so graphically as after the publication of *Crying at the Movies*.
I had written about my father's death out of a sense of need
and urgency. It was a story I had to tell, and that was my sole
aim—at least as I understood it then. Only gradually did I
realize that the very process of writing had altered my relationship to the events I described. Until this moment I had
thought of my history as fractured, broken in two, like a bone
that had snapped. There was an unbridgeable chasm between
my current reality and my past. Time before and time after
seemed so disparate and unrelated that I could see no way to
connect them, yet the act of writing accomplished this task.
    How is this possible? Again, cognitive neuroscience may
offer some clues.
    In the neuropsychological understanding of trauma (such
as the impact of my father's death), the way the brain reacts
to an overwhelming stimulus is to release the stress hormone
cortisol. Too much of this hormone prevents the hippocam-
pus, the memory-forming part of the brain, from functioning
properly. As a result, the mind not only does not "remember"
what happened, but even more importantly, it cannot form a
coherent narrative to contain this experience. The gist of this
idea is that memory and story-telling are essential to the process of making meaning. Traumatic experience, in contrast,
has no "meaning." Rather than taking its place in a larger,
ongoing narrative that includes ordinary events and experiences linked with one another in time, it stands alone, as if
proclaiming its terrible uniqueness and disconnection from

life as a whole. What characterizes trauma is endless repetition of the same or stasis.

The neuropsychology of trauma fits with my own experience in that the mental and emotional chaos I associated with my dad's death seemed to cut my life in two. I literally had no memory of his death, although I was present at the scene and must have witnessed something. My inability to compose a narrative of what happened created a schism in my history. Although I could recall events from my early childhood, they seemed completely irrelevant to everything that happened later. The memories of my early years seemed to belong to someone else. In any case, I could not make use of them in a productive way. Focusing on them for any length of time only reminded me of how much I had lost. It was as if, standing on one bank of a flood-swollen river, I could glimpse the other shore—but no way to get across.

Writing *Crying at the Movies* changed this metaphor—and reality. Almost imperceptibly, I began to feel my childhood memories returning—quietly and without fanfare—like friendly spirits or ghosts. The river was no longer wild and unbridgeable. Perhaps I experienced, for the first time in my adult life, what most people do on a day-to-day basis: the working of ordinary memory. What others may perceive as normal, hence unremarkable, to me felt miraculous. Like walking on water.

There is an analogy, I think, between the ordinary operation of memory and the process of writing. Each connects disparate aspects of thought and experience in ways that are both familiar and new. Personal memory is a primitive form of narrative, a way of reminding ourselves of what happened and how we felt, in relation to significant moments in our lives. When we recall these events, we not only revive them as once perceived and understood but also connect them to something occurring in the present. Blending old experiences with ones that are in the process of unfolding creates a new synthesis, one of memory and meaning. What the brain does—even without our conscious participation—is generate narrative, an ever-evolving sequence of storylines that help us to make sense of our lives over time. When these storylines are disrupted—as in traumatic experience—so also is our capacity to integrate and interpret, which, in turn, inhibits our ability to imagine the future. In order to live and thrive in time, we rely on the complex story-making properties of memory.

Memoir writing makes these storylines conscious and explicit, lifting them from the realm of fleeting recall into that of sustained reflection. Out of the Milky Way of neural network activity, it calls forth individual constellations. Like memory, moreover, its activity is not fixed but rather forms and re-forms itself in ceaseless flux. Once in print, words on a page stay put, but the mental activity that produces them moves restlessly forward, weaving, dissolving, and reweaving ever new designs of meaning.

Over the course of writing *Great River Road*, I pursued my private vision of pleroma—the sense of intense happiness, integration of my history, and fullness of being—that the renewed access to my childhood memories elicited. So powerful was this impetus that I hardly noticed the gradual emergence of a possibly deeper awareness. While painstakingly delineating one constellation from the Milky Way of my consciousness, another more distant cluster of stars began to appear.

Memory, like memoir writing, changes ground, even as we seek to fix it in our minds. The past only exists in the present, and the present is a kind of Proteus, a shape-shifter who cannot be seized but only momentarily apprehended. This is what I came to understand by writing about my father's death and through my extended meditation on pleroma.

The older I become, the more humble I feel about absorbing and understanding the past. I don't have a handle on it, and there's nothing I can represent as absolutely true. All I can do is record my movement through my personal memories, combined with the revelations of the ongoing present, while maintaining an open stance toward the future.

At age sixty, I began to explore the interplay between mindfulness and memory that not only configures my past, but also shapes my anticipation of the future.

The result is *Great River Road*, an extended meditation on how we make our way through our later lives, incorporating bits and pieces of the ones we've already lived, how the remembered past suffuses and enriches the present moment, and how we might imagine a life as an ongoing creation that aims toward a vision of something meaningfully integrated, if not whole.

Another way to say this is that in 2002, my life suffered a sea-change. Into something rich and strange.

Great River Road

Great River Road

Back out of all this now too much for us,
Back in a time made simple by the loss
Of detail, burned, dissolved, and broken off
—Robert Frost, "Directive"

"I've been on the road too much," I say to my brother Ron. It's late August, and I've just taken a leisurely drive down Great River Road, which snakes along the Mississippi River from Minneapolis, where I've lived for close to thirty years, to St. Louis, where Ron and I grew up. I've been telling him about the number of business trips I've taken in the last year. Being a reluctant traveler, I'm surprised to discover that I've been out of town at least once a month.

"I only realized how often I've been away from home," I say, "when I sat down and made a list. I can't believe I've done this—especially after 9/11."

"I don't like to leave home," my brother says. "I never have."

We're sitting in a bar at a restaurant called The Feasting Fox, where my parents used to go in their early married days. Back then, it had a different name—Al Smith's—the old name still inscribed under the more recent, English pub-type one on the sign outside. Not much else seems to have changed between then and now. The bar is paneled in dark wood; there's a moth-eaten stag head mounted on one wall, and the booths have plush leather seats, which feel good to sink into and create an indefinable sense of privacy. Though the restaurant doesn't seem to be doing much business, the bar scene is lively, and I suspect this is what keeps the establishment going. It's a comfortable place, where my brother and I seem to gravitate by unspoken agreement whenever I come to town.

"I'm afraid something bad will happen on a trip," Ron adds after a pause.

I'm not that surprised by my brother's pronouncement—he has often said as much—but this time I hear him in a new way. It isn't just 9/11 that is on my mind, but our family history. Something bad did happen on a trip when we were children. We watched our father drown on a boat excursion up the Mississippi River in the summer of 1951. Though I've spent years in therapy probing the far-reaching effects of this single moment in time, I've never before considered it in regard to my uneasiness about travel, which is something I feel ashamed of and don't like to admit.

છત્જ

For one thing, I have trouble reading maps. As a child I was completely mystified by them. A map looked like a field of confusion, so busy with small print and squiggly lines that I couldn't bear to look at one for long—much less figure out how to use it to get someplace I wanted to go.

As an adult, I hated driving anywhere by myself. I wasn't even eager to learn this simple mechanical skill, which most teenagers dream about long before the learner's permit age of fifteen. For me, such an opportunity held only dread. Not only was I afraid of having to find my way on my own to some destination, but I was also convinced that I was too physically uncoordinated to manage a brake and a clutch.

True to my expectation, I failed my first driver's test. I was so flustered that I missed a stop sign, made a left turn into the wrong lane of a one-way street, and did so badly on parallel parking that my examiner finally told me to stop. "You would have had an accident," he reprimanded me sharply. "I should issue you a ticket. Don't come back until you've had more practice. And for God's sake learn how to drive!"

It was all so complex—how to adjust the movements of my feet with my eyes and hands, not to mention how to sense the delicate interaction between the gas pedal and the clutch. I concentrated on learning how to deal with an automatic transmission instead. Eventually I succeeded well enough to pass the test—though not well enough to feel at ease behind the wheel.

Driving—and travel in general—made me anxious.

It wasn't always this way.

When I was very small (maybe four to six years old), I remember loving the car trips that we took as a family into the country. Every weekend, it seemed, we got into our bulbous Chevy, with front seats that stretched all the way across, and took a drive out of town to an open field where we would get out of the car, walk around and take pictures, and then drive home again, stopping on the way at the Velvet Cream with its sign in the shape of a giant vanilla cone. I was happiest when I would ride home in the front seat, softly cushioned between the bodies of my mother and father. If I was really lucky, my dad would carry me from the back alley garage into the house, snuggled warmly against his chest and shoulder. Travel, in this way, felt both exciting and safe.

It wasn't until I was well into middle age that I understood the actual purpose of these trips.

"Your father was looking for a farm to buy," my mother says in response to my reminiscing about those days, releasing a piece of information she has hoarded for nearly half a century. "That was how we wound up spending a summer in Kimmswick. He considered buying that house, but thought it was too far to commute to work. And then he decided to get a boat instead."

As if startled by where her memories are taking her, my mother falls silent. She has crossed an invisible line in her mind. Even such an oblique reference to my dad's death puts an end to her willingness to talk.

It's as though my mother has a literal roadblock in her brain, one with flashing red lights and dire warnings about the consequences of proceeding further. This roadblock has created a virtual schism between her memories of my dad and everything that came after.

I seem to have internalized the same roadblock in the process of growing up. Intuitively, I shy away from subjects that might cause my mother distress. As a result, I too am largely unable to focus on memories from my early child-hood—the period before my dad died. Being cut off from my past, however, makes it difficult for me to imagine a future. Not being able to go back in time makes it equally hard to go forward—though I do inch along, of course, day by day and year by year. Now, suddenly, in my mid-fifties, I begin to see this problem in a new light. Perhaps it has something to do with my trouble reading maps?

Eventually, I learned how to drive a stick shift—less from choice than necessity. When I married my husband, Frank, at age twenty-four, his family gave us a car as a wedding present. Without consulting me, Frank asked for a five-speed trans-mission. As long as we were going somewhere together, he could drive, but if I wanted to use the car by myself I'd have to change gears. Still feeling humiliated by my first failed effort, I delayed confronting this task until the inconvenience of being stuck at home overcame my resistance. With Frank as patient instructor, I careened around a succession of empty parking lots until I felt confident that I could manage our car on the road.

By this time, I had acquired a host of other anxieties. I avoided two-lane roads out of fear of passing in the opposing lane. If I had to pass, I would wait until the road ahead was clear as far as I could see. Only in this way would I feel sure of averting a head-on collision. I was equally frightened of the on-ramps to freeways, where the cars whizzed by so fast I couldn't believe they would actually let me in. In this case, I was anxious about being rammed from behind. Once safely entered into the stream of traffic, I would monitor the distance between me and the car in front. What if the traffic suddenly stopped? I had grisly images of multiple-car accidents. Even exiting my own driveway, I would worry over a child dashing across my path just out of my rear-view line of sight.

I didn't trust cars and trusted myself even less.

If I had to drive, I preferred taking a familiar route. I didn't like going someplace new or out of my usual circuit. If I couldn't get Frank to drive under these circumstances, I'd ask for very specific directions, which I'd carry with me in written form, in preference to consulting a map—though I would resort to one if I got completely lost.

Maps tended only to make matters worse. It would take me several minutes to orient myself in terms of north, south, east, and west, then several more minutes to locate my point of departure. By this time, I would feel a mild panic. Referring to the street guide for my destination rarely helped. Once I'd located the proper coordinates, I still had trouble finding the street in question. Even if I did, I would have to figure out how to get there from the place where I'd gotten lost. Often, I'd fold up the map in despair and look for a gas station attendant for assistance. I'd find my way at last, but by the time I arrived I'd be late, apologetic, and tense.

It was much easier staying home.

My dad liked to go places. In addition to our Sunday drives into the country, he would take us on canoe trips on the Meramec River—before buying the cabin cruiser we used to explore the wider, swifter, and deeper Mississippi. For business reasons, he also traveled by plane—in an era when passenger flight was still something of a novelty—to Maine, Florida, Washington, and California. Later, he was thrilled to cross the equator on his most extended trip—to Australia and New Zealand. For this accomplishment, he received a mock certificate from Pan American Airlines—with the figure of Jupiter seated on a cloud, holding an airplane in one outstretched hand. My dad, like Jupiter, seemed to command the space through which he moved.

Yet, he died in the midst of a trip, departing from a harbor to which he never returned.

ॐ∽

"There were stop and go lights at the entrance of the harbor," my brother muses, as our conversation dips further into the past, "because the entrance was narrow and you couldn't see around the bend. There was room for only one boat at a time."

"Funny, I'd completely forgotten that," I say, wondering how I could have obliterated such a vivid image. But, as we continue talking, I begin to feel that I do remember what Ron is telling me, as if some fragment of his reminiscence has resuscitated mine. Either that or his memory seems so real to me that I embrace it as my own. Do I truly recall this feature of the harbor, or have I cloned it from my brother? In either case, I'm sure it's true. Though only a fragment, it fits an empty space in the mental picture I am trying to assemble.

"Do you remember the first harbor where we used to dock our boat?" I ask. "I think it was called North Shore. Didn't we leave it because Dad had some kind of quarrel with the owner?"

"Yeah, and Dad was afraid he'd do something to sabotage him—like put sugar in his gas tank—so he pulled anchor and went upriver to Venetian Harbor, which was run by a guy in our neighborhood."

"Larry Wickett."

"Who died a couple of years after Dad. His wife was really broken up. She never got over it. She used to get drunk and want to cry on Mom's shoulder. Do you remember the time she came to the front door, soused out of her mind, and you and I had to get rid of her?"

Once again, I draw a blank. Why can't I remember this? "Her name was Jean, wasn't it?" Something is beginning to come back. Am I plagiarizing from my brother again? Or truly remembering?

ॐॐ

When we left Venetian Harbor on August 28, 1951—no doubt waiting for the green light that signaled us to pass into the wide channel of the river—we had no idea that we would never come back.

We cruised upriver, as usual, stopping at small towns on the Illinois side for the night. After two days, we began our leisurely descent to St. Louis. On the morning of the 30th, Dad was annoyed with my brothers and me for waking him up with our chatter. He kept a mysterious "black book," where he recorded our childish transgressions.

The boat, a forty-two-foot Richardson, was small for a family like ours. There was hardly enough space below for two bunks—for my older brother Bob and me, with a canvas stretched between them for our younger brother Ron. My parents slept above us on benches, where we ate meals during the day and which folded out at night into cots. Our accommodations were lean and tight.

Having woken up in a bad mood, Dad was out of sorts all morning. He didn't like the first sandbar where we stopped for lunch and insisted that we move to another site. Once we had settled again, his spirits seemed to improve. We chose a picnic spot on the beach and laid out our sandwiches and pop. While we were waiting the prescribed hour before going into the water—so we wouldn't get stomach cramps—my brothers and I played in the sand. At one point Dad asked me to wash his back with soap, which I did, using buckets of river water to sluice it off. I was having fun. I remember that he laughed.

At this point there's a break in the little movie I am playing in my head, as my memory sputters and then goes blank. It picks up again when my mother, two brothers, and I get back on the boat to seek help for Dad, who is nowhere to be seen in the fast moving, dirt-brown waters of the Mississippi. The river, like a giant fish, seems to have opened its maw and swallowed my father whole.

托托

"We tried to get help at a house on the river," Ron says, "but they refused, so we went on."

Once again, I am surprised by the clarity of my brother's reminiscence. Though I remember stopping at a marina upriver and waiting what seemed like hours in a trailer for someone to come from St. Louis to take us home, I have no recollection of the incident Ron describes. Did it really happen? He was only seven years old at the time. How accurate could his memory be? And why, at age nine, did I not register the same details? I hang on my brother's words, not entirely believing, but not disbelieving either. He, at least, claims to remember.

"I was used to noticing things," he says. "I was so little that no one paid attention to me. I remember how Al Hunt would bring us bags of groceries after Dad died, because Mom didn't have any cash. Then, one day, he stood in the kitchen and told her that he couldn't bring any more. Mom was really upset. Dad's will was in probate, and everything was in his name, including his bank account."

This story is new to me. I know that Al was the one who sold our boat for us, but I haven't the dimmest recollection of his supplying us with groceries.

"Was it Al who came to bring us home from the river?" I ask. "I remember flying back to St. Louis in somebody's private plane and then eating coffee cake in the kitchen with other friends of Mom and Dad."

"I don't recall that," says Ron.

❧

The year that my mother began her slow descent to death, I tried to talk with my older brother, Bob. I contacted him by phone to tell him what our mother's doctor had said on her most recent release from the hospital. The doctor advised us to consider a nursing home, which I knew Mom would never accept. My brother agreed, but didn't have any other ideas to propose. I suppose it was the imminence of our mother's death that led us into conversation about Dad, whom—observing the code of silence in our family—we rarely talked about.

"What was the name of that place where we stopped to get help?" I ask, hoping to resolve a question that has been nagging at me for years.

"Keithsburg. On the Illinois side." Bob's voice sounds rough, as if he may be trying not to cry.

"How do you spell that?" I say, cradling the phone against my ear and reaching for a pencil and a piece of paper.

"Are you taking this down? Are you going to write about this? Because if you are, I'm not going to talk to you."

"I thought it might be Davenport. I keep forgetting. I just want to remember."

"Why do you want to go over all of this again?" My brother now sounds angry. "Why can't you let it be? Get on with your life. Enjoy yourself. None of this does any good."

"I'm sorry," I say. "I didn't mean to upset you. I just never knew the name of the town, that's all."

After I hang up, it occurs to me that Bob may be impatient with me because I've asked him this before—an altogether likely possibility. I have a tendency to erase any information— such as the exact day of my dad's death—that causes me distress. Now, however, I am trying to fit the pieces of my spotty internal narrative into some semblance of a coherent story. As a part of this effort, I decide on one of my trips to St. Louis to seek out Venetian Harbor—assuming that it still exists.

A remarkably simple idea occurs to me: I can look it up in the phone book. Sure enough, there is a Venetian Harbor listed—in the town of Portage Des Sioux, a name that rings a bell. A harbor has to be on the river, I tell myself, and it can't be too far out of town. If I can make my way to Portage Des Sioux, I should be able to get to Venetian Harbor. This time, I am grateful for the assistance of a map.

I set out from my mother's house in my rental car on a mild spring day in March—not telling her where I'm going, as I don't want to upset her. The trip is easy, so much so that I am pained to think how many years I've avoided making this pilgrimage. I head west and then north on the network of interstates that direct traffic through and around the city until I exit onto the highway that leads to Portage Des Sioux. It isn't long before this highway narrows to two lanes, turning into a country road that stretches for several miles across open fields. As I near the town, I even see a sign for Venetian Harbor, as if someone had anticipated my wishes, offering me a personal guide. Making a series of turns down dirt and gravel roads, I find myself facing the scene I have carried since childhood in my imagination.

It is nothing like what I remember.

The marina before me consists of a single row of dingy-looking vessels, most of which are speedboats. Where are the extensive waterways, elaborate docks, and stately cabin cruisers I have pictured? The water is murky and stagnant, the grounds are scruffy, and the boat house is little more than a shack. The harbor's name is a cruel misnomer. Could it really have been so seedy, so paltry, when Dad was alive? Or has it simply fallen on hard times? I close my eyes and try to reconstruct the harbor in my mind, but it's no good. My shining vision, like one of Prospero's cloud-capped towers, wavers, then disperses, leaving me standing in the gritty present.

Frost's meandering journey in his poem "Directive" takes him back to an old farm site, strewn with mementos of the life that was once lived there. His goal is not the house itself but the cold spring that supplied its water. Here he discovers "a broken drinking goblet like the Grail" that is under a spell so "the wrong ones can't find it, / So can't get saved." His poem ends with a clear imperative: "Here are your waters and your watering place. / Drink and be whole again beyond confusion." This tone is so different from the rest of the poem that I'm not sure who is speaking. Is it the poet himself, who has suddenly discovered strength and purpose, or a voice from somewhere outside the poem, tendering an offer of consolation? Yet another possibility occurs to me: maybe it is just Frost trying to cheer himself up.

Whatever the case may be, I can see my own wish expressed in these lines. I've come to Venetian Harbor hoping for some kind of redemption. What I find instead is a landscape so featureless that it resembles boredom. Now that I am actually here I can't think of anything to do. Finally, I decide to walk to a spot from which I can view the entrance.

The scene is just as ordinary as before, but suddenly I see it differently—not in contrast to my childhood memories, but in the context of our family's broken narrative. This is the point from which my dad set forth, confidently expecting to return just a few days later. But he drowned instead. I am the one to complete his trip.

≈

When was it that I became less afraid of the road? Was it the year that I drove halfway across the country by myself—hugging the beautiful horizontal lines of the western interstates? Interstate 80 guided me in the spring of 1993 all the way from San Francisco to Des Moines, where I took a simple turn north onto I-35 to find my way home. Along the way, I played tapes of Bob Dylan, Boz Scaggs, Linda Ronstadt, and Maria Callas singing *La Bohème*, to keep me company and hold at bay my darker fantasies of breakdown in the desert, or rape and murder in some isolated motel.

Driving, I discovered on this trip, can be a pleasure—even a form of meditation. I'd wake up in some small town in Nevada or Utah; head for the breakfast shop for scrambled eggs, bitter coffee, and toast; then to the nearest gas station to fill my tank for the first leg of my journey. For the next seven or eight hours, I'd be my own company on the incomparably straight and smooth interstate until I arrived, several hundred miles later, at yet another western town just big enough to offer me more than one option for a night's lodging.

The landscapes that flowed past my window day after day until I was well into the Midwest had a dreamlike quality in the fine, clear air. There were mountains, then desert, then badlands, then salt flats—an ever-varying scene. The colors were a marvel: muted shades of peach, ochre, saffron, and blue-violet.

In the presence of such visual beauty, I could not feel any of my usual anxieties. Even my thoughts seemed to untangle and smooth themselves out into long, looping narratives, linking my past and present lives. Mile by mile, I seemed to be creating a multi-stranded plot, in which no detail was so jagged or anomalous that it had to be left out.

I felt comforted by the rhythms of long-distance travel. Get in the car, hit a steady speed of 70 miles per hour, and keep my eyes on the road stretching for miles in a clear sight line all the way to the horizon. Reach out with one hand to listen to the flip side of Joan Baez singing "Diamonds and Rust," or find another cassette in the bag next to me on the front seat. Stop for gas, for Cokes, for restrooms, for lunch, but keep driving until dusk, fatigue, or an especially appealing town tempts me for the night. As long as I didn't pick up any hitchhikers, I figured I was safe.

The interstates, with their wide lanes and rectangular green signs were so clearly marked that even someone as map-challenged as I couldn't get lost. I was alone but never lonely.

Trucks were my steady companions, as single-minded and goal-oriented as I. I'd pass them on upgrades only to see them whiz by me later. When I hit a stretch of bad weather—as I did in Wyoming in a patch of sleet turning to snow—I'd be grateful to ride behind them, letting them scout the territory ahead. They were like bodyguards, shielding me from the worst effects of the storm.

For the first time, I understood why Americans are so much in love with the automobile. By this time as well, I had my own stick shift car. After I'd finally learned to drive one, I took some pride in the feeling of control it gave me. Automatic transmissions were for sissies, I thought. But the most important thing about this solo trip across country was the fact of my doing it with no wrong turns, no accidents, no encounters with sexual harassers, much less serial killers. I had covered two thousand miles without incident.

ॐॐ

As the evening deepens in the bar of the Feasting Fox, so does my conversation with my brother Ron. We're both on our third round of drinks and oblivious to the bustle around us— this being the first time we've shared our memories of the day of our father's death.

"I can't remember anything about the accident," I say. "I really don't understand what happened."

"Well, Bob was boasting about how far he could swim," Ron begins. "And Dad told him to swim out to a stick that was floating by in the water. So he did. But the current was fast, and the stick was also moving fast. Bob went too far and panicked. He kept raising his hand for help—because you remember how Dad used to warn us about 'crying wolf.' Finally, Mom realized what was going on and told Dad to get out there and do something."

I'm mesmerized by Ron's story. Not just the details of it, but its certainty—and the confidence he has in the telling. How can his memory be so much better than mine?

"Mom and Dad got into an argument about who was at fault. Then she said, 'He's your son, you go rescue him.'"

Can this be true? Did my parents actually quarrel over the fate of their son? If so, how much time did they lose in this way? I'm so shocked by my brother's revelation that I can't think of anything to say.

"Dad went after him and pushed him toward shore. Mom waded in to pull him out."

My older brother has told me about Dad's rescuing him, but not about the stick in the water or the unseemly fight on the beach. In his account, Dad is a hero, risking (and losing) his own life to save that of his son. In a letter to Bob not long afterwards, one of our dad's Jesuit friends even compares his sacrifice to that of Christ. "There is no greater love," he says, without qualification. Ron offers another set of possible motivations. What about fear or shame?

"He did a foolish thing," I say at last, "telling Bob to swim after a stick." Suddenly, I feel very tired. "Let's go home," I say, signaling to our waiter for the check.

The father I have loved and idealized for my entire life now appears to me in another light. At first, I feel furious with him—for giving Bob such a stupid instruction, as if he were a dog ordered to go fetch. And then for not being strong or clever enough to resist the terrible current of the river, the very thing he had warned us kids about. So he was human after all, not the god-like figure I had enshrined in my memory. Yet, he did save my brother's life, and paid for this selfless act with his own. For a while, I hold two views of him in my mind, unable to choose between them. I even begin to doubt Ron's story. Perhaps he is splicing two reminiscences together?

My parents were both rather hot-tempered and had lots of arguments, many of which I witnessed as a child. Maybe Ron's way of coping with the intolerable nature of what happened on the beach is to create a story that explains it? On the other hand, he may have been so riveted to the drama playing itself out in front of him that he recorded it—as he has other things I don't recall—more or less verbatim. Finally, I give up trying to resolve this question. Ron sticks to his version of the story, Bob won't talk, and I can't remember. Our mother, the person most likely to be able to shed some light on this mystery, never once breaks her silence about it. Since I am too scared to ask, she carries her forbidden knowledge to the grave.

∞

Gradually, in mid-life, I make my peace with roads. So it is that in August of 2002, I decide to take a driving trip to St. Louis—this time forsaking the comforting interstates to follow a patchwork of interconnecting roads, coinciding for the most part with Highway 61, which hugs the shoreline of the Mississippi River. This sinuous route, officially designated as the Great River Road, is marked by signs in the shape of a steamboat steering wheel all the way from Minnesota to Louisiana. Though I have driven this way once before, it was with a companion who navigated our course. This time, I try it on my own.

At first, I'm as frightened as I used to be about losing my way and take several wrong turns—crossing a bridge into Wisconsin before I realize that I'm following a sign that points east instead of west. I pull over, consult my map, and realize that I can cross back into Iowa further downstream. I take this slight deviation as an opportunity to relax and explore, stopping at each historical marker along the way.

Back in Iowa, I encounter a dreamscape of rolling hills, grasses, and fields high above the river. Driving the crest of the river bluffs gives me a timeless feeling, as if I could follow this road indefinitely into a space that exists nowhere and belongs to no one. It is as close to my imagination of heaven as I have ever come.

Toward dusk, I leave this beautiful section of the road and descend into industrial Clinton, where I get lost once again. Cities of any size confuse me. Whereas the interstates will speed you through or around them, the local highways are indistinguishable from ordinary city streets. In Clinton, I try to follow the signs for the Great River Road but find myself in a maze instead. Tired and discouraged, I pull over to a gas station and open my map. A truck pulls in next to me, and a woman in a silver Dodge Caravan looks over to ask if I need help. A younger man with blond dreadlocks sits by her side, and both look sympathetic. I tell them that I am trying to find a motel for the night, and he says that they are "a long way out."

"Follow me," the woman says, "and we'll guide you there."

Gratefully, I do, until they pull over near a strip of motel lodgings. I thank them, as they make a quick U-turn and depart. I take the first motel in sight, which looks pretty good on the outside but is dirty and tattered within. There are cigarette butts on the worn carpet leading to my room, and the curtains that shield me from the fluorescent light along the corridor are torn, but I'm too tired to go back to the main office and make a change.

In the morning when I step outside, I am aware of a rotten smell so nauseating that I want to hold my breath. In the gas station, I ask the cashier if she knows what this is about. "Oh," she says, "that would be the corn processing. There's a plant down the road a ways, on the river."

Unlike the interstates, which don't allow you to experience a city with any degree of intimacy, the Great River Road takes you to its heart. You will first moderate your speed from 55 to 45, then 35 miles per hour, and suddenly you will find yourself on Main Street, braking for every stoplight. Some towns, like Bellevue, Iowa, which features a park that runs the length of the highway and the river, are a visual delight, while others, such as Clinton, make you want to escape. Not only does the road fail to direct you in a straight line to your destination, it also offers a hodge-podge of impressions. Given an option, I'd choose Bellevue, but Clinton is also a part of the deal I've made by taking this route.

On my way home from St. Louis, I decide to follow the east side of the river to see the parts of Illinois and Wisconsin that

I missed on the way down. By this point, I feel more confident about getting where I want to go—regardless of wrong turns. I also want to find Keithsburg, the place where my mother, two brothers, and I left our boat—along with our life as we had known it until August 30, 1951.

This trip takes me two days, Keithsburg being farther north than I had imagined and not even on the Great River Road. However, I get close enough this way to find a network of smaller roads, like tiny capillaries, hardly even discernible on my map, that takes me there. More than once, I get out of my car at some lonely crossroad with a single café or gas station to ask directions. Each time, I wind my way closer to the water—until finally I drive onto a gravel road that descends slowly to a boat landing at the river's edge.

By now, it's mid-afternoon on a hot summer's day—not much activity at this hour. Yet, I can see from the few boats offshore that small craft enter the water here—mostly speedboats, though there is also a houseboat swaying at anchor. I swiftly scan the area. To the south, there is some kind of inlet, formed by a woody outcropping of land that looks vaguely familiar. Directly in front of me lies the wide and glittering expanse of the Mississippi.

Have I been here before, as Bob tells me? I believe that I have, feeling as if I'm immersed in a recurring dream. I seem to recognize the configuration of beach, land spit, water, and cottonwood trees before my eyes. Even the sign reading "Public Boat Launch" looks familiar—though its lettering and iconography must be recent.

To the north (upriver), I notice a trailer campsite, looking as if it had been preserved in amber since the 1950s. Can my childhood memory of waiting in someone's trailer on the day of my dad's death possibly be accurate? A single road runs through this camp, which I follow, as if guided by an insistent memory trace. "Maybe," I think, "just maybe." On the other side, I enter another uncanny scene—as if some divine hand had conjured it from my long-ago, girlhood experience.

A rectangular sign, painted white with block lettering, reads KEITHSBURG BOAT CLUB. This "club" consists of a single-story, wood-frame building with two rooms, one of which contains a bar that overlooks the water. Outside, there is a newer looking open shelter, painted barn red, with picnic tables underneath.

It's as if I have walked onto a movie set designed specifically for me. Though the picnic area looks contemporary, it has the feel of an earlier era. The Boat Club is vintage, like an aging but beloved relative whose wrinkles, rheumatic hands, and silver hair are tokens of a life fully lived. So what if it looks a little rickety, lacks paint, or slouches down toward the water. Anything built near the Mississippi is married to it, so to speak. In this case, successive floods have clearly taken their toll—the most recent of which is documented by a sign halfway up one side of the building, marking the place where the river crested in the spring of 1993.

If I listen carefully, I can almost hear my dad striking up a conversation in the bar over a beer or two, while I stand by his side, shyly ordering a cream soda for myself. I can imagine our family having barbecued ribs and French fries at one of the Formica tables in the middle of the room. Could we have stopped here for the night before moving downriver? And returned to the nearest place where we hoped to find help? The Keithsburg Boat Club makes this wisp of a memory feel real.

I open the screen door to a room that looks like a kitchen and continue into the bar area, populated on this lazy Saturday afternoon by a few men. As the only woman in the room, I feel conspicuous, but I'm determined to go forward. Summoning my courage, I walk up to the bar.

"I'm wondering if you can help me. I'm looking for someone who knows when this club was established. My family used to have a boat, and I think we may have stopped here once."

"Well, little lady," the bartender says with exaggerated courtesy, "I don't know myself. I'm a newcomer to this area. But there's some in this room who might be able to help. Herb here, for instance, is a real old-timer." He nods and points to a man in a button-down, short-sleeved shirt, who is sitting at the far end of the bar and who catches my eye as I turn to face him. Other eyes are trained on me also, as I thank the bartender and make my way toward the man he has designated. Not much going on today, other than a baseball game on TV. A woman in this male preserve—even one who is obviously middle-aged—stirs interest.

Herb scrapes his stool aside to make room for me to sit. I take the place next to him.

"Everything looks so familiar. I was wondering if this club goes back to the '50s."

"Don't believe so," Herb says, looking at me appraisingly. "I'm sixty-five—prob'ly the oldest one here. These young'uns"—he catches the eye of the bartender and winks— "don't go back far enough to remember."

"Have you lived here long?"

"Used to live on the other side of the river but the wife and me moved over to this side after Jackie—that's our daughter— was born. My wife wanted to be closer to her family was the reason."

"When was that? I mean when you moved?"

"Sometime in the early '60s. Don't know that it made such a difference—in terms of family. They wasn't that close to begin with. And the wife died not long after."

"I'm sorry," I say, suddenly abashed. I hadn't bargained on someone else's story of loss. I look down at my hands as Herb picks up his glass and makes a coughing sound in his throat.

"You know, I could be wrong," I say, trying to catch his eyes to express sympathy. "We used to stop on both sides of the river. Maybe I'm thinking of someplace else."

"Might could," Herb says. "Sorry I'm not more help."

"But you've been so kind," I say, not knowing how to end this conversation, yet also at a loss about how to go on.

I stand awkwardly and hold out my hand for a goodbye.

"My pleasure." A big hand takes mine and holds it warmly. "Not ever' day I get to talk to a pretty woman like you."

Herb and I are close enough in age for his comment to make me blush. To cover my embarrassment, I smile and thank him again as I turn and walk away.

I was so sure. How could I experience such a rush of pure bodily sensation if I were wrong? Yet, the only form of evidence I have tells me just that. This perfect, movie-set, vintage club did not exist in the summer of 1951. Or did it? None of the men in the bar was there at the time. How could they know? As I drive through town, I decide to find the local historical society, signs for which I've noticed in passing on my way to the river.

When I get there, I find the building locked. It's Saturday, and no one is in sight. I knock on the door and peer through the windows, hoping that someone (perhaps a maintenance person) might be lurking within. No such luck. I can't imagine staying around for another two nights until business hours resume on Monday. This particular mystery will remain unresolved.

But then, who cares? It matters only to me. And I'm not even sure how much it matters that I've found the actual place where my family anchored our boat for a night, where my dad had a few beers in the bar, and where we all ate barbecued ribs and French fries at a Formica table as a family—before we became something else.

Maybe the important thing is that I feel so at home here—in this border-river town, neglected by time and virtually all traffic routes, including the Great River Road. I've discovered a place where what happened, what might have happened, and what I am experiencing in the present somehow coincide. In Keithsburg, the deep past feels as real as the simmering August day when I revisit it. Both are present for me simultaneously, conversing for the first time in my life with each other.

Reunion

A landscape does not have to involve land. Time is a
landscape.
> —Andy Goldsworthy

In the spring of 1993, I fly to St. Louis to attend the first
reunion of my grade-school class. It's been thirty-seven
years since we graduated from Immaculate Conception, a
kindergarten through eighth-grade parish school, and we're
all in our early fifties. Though we've scattered over the years,
most of us still live in the greater St. Louis area. I'm one of a
handful who left the state.

A lot has changed in the old neighborhood. Interstate 44,
one of the first federal highways authorized by the National
Interstate and Defense Highways Act signed by Eisenhower in
1956 (the year we all graduated high school), has bisected the
parish, severing the poorer residents to the north from their
near neighbors to the south. The church and school, located
on the north side of the interstate, have had a hard time of it
since. In the years I've been coming back to visit my mother, I

have sometimes driven through this area, witnessing the decline, closing, and vandalization of the school. I've also seen sturdy brick houses disappear only to be replaced by weedy, empty lots. In the midst of this devastation, Immaculate Conception Church, a neo-Gothic limestone structure, remains massively intact.

The reunion begins at IC Church, where we meet for five o'clock Mass before going to dinner at Garavelli's, a popular, family-run restaurant on the south side. I'm nervous, as I've avoided going to church for most of my adult life. Not knowing whether I should take a hat—though I never wear one—I drape a scarf over my dress, thinking I can use it to cover my hair, if necessary. But I'll have to wing it in terms of the service, the specifics of which I've long since forgotten.

I'm surprised by how many people greet me in the vestibule, calling me by my nickname. I recognize the popular in-crowd from the old days: Lois Ottenad, Rosalie Gage, and Pat Manzelli (the organizers of the reunion), along with guys I used to admire from afar: Richard Gutierrez, Tom Komadina, and Dennis Rabbitt. Lois, Rosalie, and Pat all knew where to shop and wore ballerina flats and hoop skirts long before I did. Richard, Tom, and Dennis were altar boys, but they also played hooky and hung out at Wilde's Drug Store down the street from church. I had a special place in my heart for Rich, whose dark, good looks made me think of Tony Curtis in *The Prince Who Was a Thief*.

Out of a class of twenty-eight, twenty-four of us are here—a remarkable showing after all this time. "How are you? How good to see you. You look wonderful," I say over and over amidst handshakes and light hugs.

Still greeting each other, we move into the church and fill the pews. Shouldn't we stop talking, I wonder, remembering how the Sisters used to shush us with disapproving looks. I'm more at sea than I expected.

An elderly priest enters, not only facing us but speaking to us directly. Another shock. In my memory, priests faced the altar, turned away from the congregation.

"I'm Father Gavin," he begins. "I wasn't here when your class graduated, and I'm sure you've noticed changes in the neighborhood. We merged with St. Henry's in the 1970s. Our congregation is small, but we're still here. I'm a member of the Augustinian order and a guest pastor for this church. Hopefully the diocese will decide to maintain this parish when the assistant pastor and I retire."

Father Gavin's stooped frame and silver hair underscore his point. I had no idea the parish was so endangered.

"We serve a lot of recent immigrants—Southeast Asians, mostly, but also a lot of African-Americans—and we think this church performs a vital function in the community. I hope you agree. Welcome back, and enjoy your reunion!"

As Mass begins, Father Gavin continues to face us and to speak in English. Clearly I've missed something in all the years I've been away—something related to Vatican II, no doubt. I look around, taking cues from my classmates, all of whom seem to know what to do. When they stand, I stand. When they kneel, I kneel. When they say something I can't follow, I bow my head in silence. As the service unfolds, my astonishment increases.

One of my female classmates gets up to read the first passage from the liturgy. I'm so nonplussed—when I was a child only priests were allowed to do this—that I gaze at her open-mouthed. Then another classmate—my old friend Margo, the only one of us to have entered and stayed in a religious order—mounts the pulpit for a second reading. I'm now completely out of step and try to conceal my embarrassment, as it seems I alone am confused.

Father Gavin tells us to offer a sign of peace to one another—a gesture that has no meaning for me until the person to my right extends her hand and reaches for mine. I swing to my left and do the same. When I turn around, the man behind me leans forward to embrace me. This is Joe Judge, whom I considered the handsomest boy in our eighth-grade class. "Peace be with you," he says, lightly touching my shoulders. "Peace to you," I say in return.

What on earth will I do when it comes to Communion? I haven't been to Confession in over thirty years, and, being divorced, I am surely in a state of sin. Yet, I don't want to call attention to myself. As my classmates move forward, row after row, to receive the Eucharist, I follow. To hold back would only make me conspicuous.

I now face a new dilemma. No one kneels, as we did as children at the altar railing, with eyes closed, extending our pink tongues. Rather, we walk single file towards Father Gavin, with hands cupped to receive the wafer placed there firmly by him or one of his assistants—grown-up lay people judging by their dress—who move forward from one side of the altar. No boys in black cassocks with white crocheted blouses here! Other men and women hold goblets from which some communicants bow their heads to take a sip. By now, I am completely disoriented, so I decline the cup, meekly following my pew mates back to my seat.

Many things about the church look the same: the gothic arches; the enormous crucifix above the altar; the life-size statues of Jesus, Mary, and Joseph; the dark-wood confessionals; stained-glass windows; and sculpted Stations of the Cross. Even the linoleum tiles—waxy yellow and dark red—are reassuringly familiar. But what to make of the ritual? In outline it is the same, but everything feels strange—more Protestant than Catholic somehow. Yet, my classmates appear to be at ease in the midst of this sea-change. Have they been churchgoers all these years? Am I the only one who has not kept faith?

As children, we don't question what our parents or teachers tell us about the world and how it works—unless there's a reason. My dad's death was such a reason. Until then, I felt pretty much at home in my family, school, church, and neighborhood. I loved my parents, did well in school, played rough-and-tumble with my two brothers, had a best girlfriend who lived across the street, and a boyfriend who lived down the block. Why should I not trust the stories I heard about God, who made this benign universe; his son Jesus, who suffered out of kind and good intentions; his mother Mary, who adored her baby the way any mother should; my personal guardian angel, who followed me everywhere protecting me from terrible accidents; and a ghost who was more holy than frightening? Stories that explained everything.

Yet, not one part of this beautiful construction made sense to me after my dad's death. How could I care about God's family when my own was destroyed? As hard as I tried, I could not picture heaven as a real place, where my father waited for me in clouds of eternity. Instead, time was what I knew—a succession of dreary days, each as gray and empty as the last. When I first read *Macbeth* in high school, I understood his view of life as an endless series of tomorrows. Like Macbeth, I had lost a world of meaning. I, too, was a walking shadow.

At age nine, however, I had no way to say any of these things, so I continued to go to church, confess my sins, take communion, sing in the choir, and memorize my catechism. At the urging of Sister Marie Fidelis in the seventh grade, I even considered the possibility of a vocation. But when I asked God to speak to me, no one answered. When I tried to quiet my mind to listen—as Sister Fidelis instructed—I heard only the echo of my own thoughts. If God had a plan for me, as my friend Margo believed he did for her, he was keeping it a mystery.

Margo, who entered the convent right out of grade school, is the only classmate I've stayed in touch with. After my dad's death, my old friends drifted away. I didn't know what to say to them. Our family's tragedy was so enormous that I was afraid it would overwhelm me if I tried to talk about it. Either that or I would start to cry and not be able to stop. Over time, I began to feel like an outcast—as if my bad luck were contagious, like the lepers we read about that only the saintly Father Damian would touch. Margo was the one friend I felt comfortable with, perhaps because she was shy and serious like me.

Sometime in sixth grade Margo and I began to walk home after school, talking about boys and clothes and planning what to do on Saturday afternoon. In the winter, I'd go over to her house, where we'd play Clue or Monopoly on a card table in her living room while her mother made popcorn for us in the kitchen. At times like these, I'd feel warm and cozy, forgetting the sadness that pervaded my own home. One year her father, who was a policeman, invited us to a Christmas party for children who lived in his precinct. We sang carols, received gift packages from Santa, and sucked orange juice through peppermint-stick straws.

In the summers, I went with Margo and her parents to a cabin they were building in the country, where we'd tromp through the woods trying to decide what we wanted to be when we grew up. I had dim notions of going to college, but I also thought that being a secretary was glamorous. Margo seemed torn between marrying her second cousin—a daring boy whom we both admired—or becoming a nun. At night, after hot dogs and roasted marshmallows, we'd whisper secrets to each other from our bunk beds.

I liked Margo because she laughed easily, exclaiming "Oh, Lord!" and "Oh, kid!" as if I were a normal child like her—someone with two parents.

Margo's mother, a diminutive woman with granny glasses and marcelled hair, was not beautiful to my eyes (not like my own mother that is), but she was always glad to see me, welcoming me with a big hug and asking about my family. Like Margo, she was religious, going to Mass with her daughter on weekdays before school—as the nuns told us to do—which my brothers and I rarely did. Margo and her mother also wore identical medals of the Blessed Virgin on beaded, silver chains around their necks. They were holy in a way I didn't understand but which felt comforting.

When I see Margo at the reunion, I feel a rush of pleasure. She's shorter and plumper than I recall, but her face, framed by a black veil with a starched white brim, looks as soft and kind as ever. The last time we met in the mid-'80s, she was in lay dress, having taken a leave of absence from her order to care for her mother, who was dying slowly from Parkinson's. Sometime in the '60s or '70s (I'm ashamed to say I don't remember which), her father was killed by a drunk driver who crossed the median line of a highway directly into his path. Her mother had only Margo to care for her when she became disabled. By then, she was living in the country in the cabin that had long since been finished, where I visited them one spring.

Margo is my idea of a good person, not because she's a nun, but because of her generous nature. Our conversations, grown-up now, are frank. On my trip to the country, where we take a long walk through the greening woods, I tell Margo about my separation, divorce, and remarriage—a painful history, much of which I'm not proud of. Margo confides her fear about her mother's rapid decline—by now, she can barely swallow, much less talk—and her anxiety about caring for her at home. "I'm afraid of an emergency," she says, "but I know that Mom is more comfortable with me than in a nursing home. And I want to be with her when she passes on."

Until now, I've been congratulating myself on helping my own mother with her various medical appointments and hospitalizations, but spending a day with Margo, watching her spoon feed her mother and patiently decipher her murmuring speech, makes me aware of how little I am willing to sacrifice. I know I would not want to give up my job or way of life to take care of my mother in her last illness.

"The Lord be with you," Father Gavin says, raising his hand to bless us with the sign of the cross. "And also with you," we reply, as a wisp of vanished Latin, *Et cum spiritu tuo,* rises to my lips. "Mass is ended," Father Gavin says. "Go in peace."

At Garavelli's, where we mingle over cocktails, I am surprised by how comfortable I feel in this group. Guys who seemed diffident to me in class or on the playground approach me with broad smiles and bear hugs. Women, whose social cliques I once felt excluded from, pepper me with questions, eager to talk. Something binds us, despite our divergent lives, our long absence, and silence. Does it have to do with learning to read and write together, living in the same neighborhood, or going to the same church? Or the smell of white glue, wet wool coats in the cupboard, waxy crayons, and chalk dust? Or perhaps the memory of Billy Finnegan being chased around the room by an exasperated Sister Ignatius, or Father Meissner's Confirmation class, punctuated by his slow, rumbling belch?

Not one of us fails the reunion quiz. *What were the school colors?* Blue and white. *Who was Pope in 1956?* Pius XII. *Who was President?* Ike. *What did we sell at Thanksgiving?* Turkey chances. *On St. Patrick's Day?* Green carnations. *Which priest left the parish to become a missionary in Bolivia?* Father Schierhoff. *Which one joined the Air Force?* Father Krieger. *Who got shot in the leg at early morning Mass?* Also Father Schierhoff. *Whose bakery supplied pastries for first Friday breakfast?* Ottenad's. *Who had the shortest last name?* Margo Rey. *Where did we go for school picnics?* The Highlands and Chain of Rocks Park.

One memory leads to another, prompted in part by a group of photos assembled on a long table covered by a white cloth.

Here we are in kindergarten in Sister Mary Donald's class with the wooden playhouse, trucks, dolls, and games. Lois, in her neat, blonde pigtails, stands to one side of the playhouse door, while my best friend, Janet Rothenheber, in a ruffled pinafore her mother made, stands on the other. The rest of us sit cross-legged on the floor, some of us holding picture books. I recognize Michael De Francisco, whose father owned a bar called Club L; Janice and Daryl Siebold, who were twins; Margo, with her hair in a bowl cut; Carol Anderson, whose mother died in a car accident in fourth grade; Pat Ohlman, the first girl to get her period; Mary Ann Azar, who introduced us to Johnny Mathis and Nat King Cole; my heartthrob, Richard Gutierrez; and Carl Zinsser, a smart, nervous boy who went on to get a PhD in engineering.

Unremarkable in my mussy hair and puffy-sleeved dress, I look directly into the eye of the camera, unaware of the tragedy that awaits my family four years later.

At our first Communion, we are assembled at the front of IC Church in our white veils and dresses with white missals, patent leather shoes, fresh haircuts, and white suits. Our solemn expressions reflect our newly acquired knowledge of sin and responsibility. Now that we've received Christ into our hearts, we must bear the burden of his suffering, along with his promise of salvation.

Our graduation photo is composite—an assemblage of single cameo shots with the image of our pastor, Father James Johnston, at the top. Already, we seem about to disperse, poised to spring into various lives and fates.

Over dinner, we share capsule histories. Most of us attended Catholic high schools, then community college or St. Louis University, the mid-town Jesuit institution where my parents met. A number of the men went into the army, pre-Vietnam, continuing their education when they got out. The women married young and had babies while working to supplement the family income. As a group, we are politically moderate and financially comfortable but not rich. A few of us have divorced, but no one else, as far as I can tell has left the Church—with the possible exception of Arthur Freund, whose bio says he has become an evangelical Christian and minister of a small congregation in Idaho. Arthur sends greetings but is too busy with pastoral duties to join us for the reunion.

The next day, I meet with Margo at the Sacred Heart Convent, where she teaches primary school children in the Italian neighborhood known as "The Hill." The convent, a Romanesque-style building with modern school wings attached, occupies a full city block, its boundaries marked by a wrought-iron fence. An elderly nun answers my ring, inviting me into a cool, tiled hallway, where I wait for her to summon Margo.

"I'm so happy you're here," Margo exclaims when she sees me. "I was so hoping you'd come to the reunion."

"I'm happy too," I say and am pleased to realize it's true.

I feel at ease with Margo despite our differences. She is less than five feet tall, while I am close to six. "Look at us," she likes to exclaim. "We're like Mutt and Jeff!" Margo entered the convent at fourteen, while I've staked a shaky claim in the world—marrying and divorcing twice and somehow managing to raise a child in the process. Margo's parents are now both deceased, while my mother—in her late seventies—struggles with heart failure, diabetes, and emphysema. Above all, Margo's faith is (or appears to be) intact, while mine is all but nonexistent.

I plan on taking Margo to Shaw's Garden, the estate of a nineteenth-century naturalist who traveled the world collecting and cultivating exotic species of plants. The Missouri Botanic Garden—as it's now called—is a public park, with extensive greenhouses, ponds, streams, and pathways covering several acres. It's one of the city's treasures, though one that I failed to appreciate as a child when forced to accompany my mother there with a steady flow of out-of-town guests. Then, the walkways seemed labyrinthine, the greenery lush but unremarkable, the flowers pale and drooping in the hot summer sun.

Today, I am grateful for the mild weather and am happily anticipating the show of early spring flowers: tulips, daffodils, hyacinths, forsythias, and azaleas. In Minneapolis these blossoms arrive much later and last only a couple of weeks. At home, mounds of hard-packed, dirty snow still line the sidewalks.

After lunch in the airy cafeteria of the new Visitor Center, we set out to explore the grounds. We wander past the old, foggy-paned greenhouses harboring giant tropical plants and into a series of herb gardens, leading slowly to larger bowers and wider paths. As we approach the Japanese garden with its gracefully arched footbridges fringed with blue irises, Margo begins to talk about her mother's death.

"I had to take her to the hospital," she says, "but I came every day, and towards the end I stayed overnight on a cot. The sisters were all so kind, but there wasn't much they could do. Mom was really ready to go by then."

Having lived in fear of death and dying, I am eager to hear how Margo coped with this experience. I think she is brave for facing it.

"I told her that I love her. And when I could see she was going, I held her hand. 'You'll be with God,' I said. 'And you'll see Dad. We'll meet again behind the golden door.'"

What kind of God does Margo imagine? What possible reunion? The idea of the Resurrection is completely implausible to me, if only on the grounds that we die so randomly and unpredictably. Were I to encounter my own father now—so much older than he was when he drowned—how would we greet each other? Could he even recognize me in middle age, when what he left was a nine-year-old girl? How could I recognize him, bloated and disfigured as he was by the time his body was found?

At IC, we were taught that God pulls bones and flesh from the earth at the Last Judgment in a physical Resurrection. I can't imagine such a process as anything other than grotesque. But I don't want to say this to Margo, who seems to take consolation from the assurance that she will be reunited with her mother and father when she dies. And who am I to say? Unlike me, Margo had the courage to nurse her mother through her long illness and witness her last breath.

I touch Margo's arm in sympathy as a group of noisy children pushes past us on the gravel path. When we arrive at a wooden bench, I suggest that we sit down for a moment to enjoy the view of the water and the sun.

The next thing Margo says takes me off guard.

"I can't tell you how depressed I was. I was feeling so bad that I didn't want to talk to anybody, didn't even want to get up in the morning. Though I would, because the children would be there every day, needing me. Finally, the Sisters sent me on retreat for group therapy; they were so worried. But I hated it. I couldn't stand talking about my mother with a group of total strangers."

I'm a believer in the value of expressing feeling, no matter how difficult, but Margo's anguish rings true to me.

"I know they meant well," she says, "but it just wasn't right for me. I finally told them I'd rather go back to work."

I don't know what to say, so I listen quietly.

"Once I'd decided to leave, I felt better. Everyone was so nice there, but I wanted to go back to the convent. Someone drove me to the train station. It was across a field that had just been ploughed for spring planting, and I was feeling pretty bad—like I'd failed some kind of test and the Sisters would be disappointed in me. I was worrying about what they would think when they saw me coming home ahead of time."

"Shall we walk?" I say, feeling suddenly restless. Margo's story about her mother's death reminds me of my own unresolved mourning for my father. How can I help her if I can't help myself?

"But you know, something wonderful happened on that drive. I was just looking out of the window when all of a sudden I saw something out of the corner of my eye. It was a bird that rose up from the field—a big, white bird, like a heron or a seagull. It floated and hovered there for a moment on the edge of my vision. And then it vanished. I asked the Sister who was with me if she had seen it too, but she said no."

"Some kind of message?"

"An epiphany."

"Your mom?"

"There's no other explanation. A bird like that didn't belong in that field. I'm sure it was a sign."

One part of me is pleased for Margo. She's been through a big ordeal—one that I will confront when my own mother dies—and I'm glad that she has found a way through it. I even admire the strength of her conviction that the bird she saw was real and that it manifested her mother's spirit. But I'm a doubter at heart. At the same time, I don't want to challenge her. On yet another, more obscure level, I wish I could believe as simply as Margo does. It makes me happy that she feels consoled in her grief, and I want to share her consolation.

So we continue walking quietly through the garden, stopping occasionally to admire a pretty vista, some delicate blossom, or new green shoots.

Margo believes in other signs and miracles—like the appearance of the Virgin at Fatima, Guadeloupe, Lourdes, and Medjugorje. In school, we were taught that Mary regularly came down from heaven to show herself, even to children like us. Why she came was less obvious. Either she had a secret message to deliver to the Pope, which he would reveal at a future date, or she wanted to establish a shrine where people who were sick could come to be cured—or she just wanted to offer hope to the poor and downtrodden. For Margo, these visitations are literal, and they arouse feelings of awe. The appearance of the white bird is similar; it's her personal experience of the divine.

I come to the end of my afternoon walk with Margo, respectful of the kind of faith I see in her—one that allows her to perceive signs and wonders in the everyday world. I also come away curious about how my other classmates have responded to our Catholic upbringing. It seems rare, these days, for a group of children to spend nine years together in the same neighborhood, sharing the same religious instruction.

Armed with my reunion booklet, I write to my classmates when I get home to Minneapolis, telling them I'm thinking about writing an article about IC and asking if they'd like to be interviewed. Many show interest, and a few respond with enthusiasm. On my next trip to St. Louis, I arrange to meet with a small group at my mother's house. By this time, my mother's health has worsened, and she's on oxygen, but she says it's all right for us to meet in the front room, so I go ahead with my plan.

Dave Schmerber, Richard Gutierrez, and Rosalie Gage arrive precisely at 7:00 p.m. Dave is a middle-level business manager, Rich is retired, and Rosalie works in an office of the Archdiocese. A small but willing sample.

I have no experience interviewing but have bought a micro-cassette tape recorder in anticipation of the evening. I take care to read the instructions and set the recorder on a coffee table that is equidistant from the three armchairs and the settee. I've stocked up on beer and wine, but no one wants anything stronger than a Coke. We spend about an hour recalling odd bits of our archaic Catholic childhood. At last, the conversation comes to rest on the issue of how Dave and Rich became altar boys.

"We were fifth-graders," Dave says. "Sixth, seventh, and eighth graders were in the altar boys—so it was something that you kind of wanted to be. And I don't know, did we start in the fourth grade with the prayers?"

"Prayers, yeah," Rich says. "Wasn't Schierhoff the guy who was teaching us?"

"And during the school year, wasn't that like on a Friday afternoon that we went to church, and we would sit in the pews at church and study the Latin?"

"Could've been. I know you had to learn these hand signals. Father would do a certain thing, put his hand up—"

"And that was the time you had to get up and get the hosts and things and—"

"One guy had the little dish and the cruet with the water, and the other guy had the towel. Some of the priests, they'd wipe their hands off, they'd fold the towel—"

"And they'd hand it to you or put it on your arm."

"But Monsignor would go whssst—"

"And you'd have to catch it. You had to be aware."

All of this is new to me, as there were no altar girls in my day. I'm surprised by the detail of Dave's and Rich's reminiscences—and also by the pleasure they're getting out of remembering.

"You had to light the candles," Rich continues, "and we used to have to do perpetual devotions."

"Tuesday nights."

"And you had to put charcoal in the censor, and it'd be in there smoldering. It'd get hot. And then comes the time for the incense, so you had to have the chain in one hand and lift the lid off—"

"That thing was really hot!"

"Father would sprinkle the incense on—and in the processions, you'd walk around swinging the incense."

"Every once in a while I still like incense, and I still love candles," Dave confesses.

"Un-huh."

"Sometimes, when the wife's not around, I light the candles, and I'll light some incense, and someone will come in and say, 'Oh, Catholic church again, huh?'"

"Whatever works," Rose says, as we all laugh.

I'm loving this conversation—I am finally getting to know my classmates who seemed so mysterious and remote to me as a child. But I'm also interested in how they view the world as adults.

"Was there a time in any of your lives when you just stopped going to church or moved away from that altogether?" I ask.

Dave admits that he stopped when he was in the service, which exposed him to different cultures, especially in Europe. Rich confesses that he got lazy after he married but went back once he started having children. "You couldn't expect your kids to go if you didn't," he states pragmatically.

Rose steps up to the plate. "I've gone continuously," she says.

What follows nearly dumfounds me.

"I can only speak for myself, but I would have to say that the Church influenced me to stay in a marriage for twenty-seven and a half years that I probably should have left the very first week. I was taught you married, and you married for life, no matter what. So I stayed and kept thinking things would get better, and it wasn't all that bad. And the children started coming—I had five children in ten years—and I tried to raise them to the best of my ability, but after a while I realized that things were going nowhere, and yet, I stayed in this marriage because of my faith. I was very involved in the parish and all my children's schools. They all went to Catholic grade schools and high schools and, in some cases, college. But it finally took a priest suggesting to me when I was on retreat for counseling that I should get a divorce.

"A priest advised you to do that?" I say in amazement.

"I guess that sounds like it's contrary to what they should be saying, but really it isn't, because there are certain situations that you should not stay in, in a marriage. More than one priest said this to me. Finally, things just escalated to the point where one day I said, 'this is it. Either I get out of this situation, or I go down the tubes.'"

"What I felt," Dave intervenes, "is that you get a divorce and take your chances. So I divorced and remarried—a non-Catholic—and we've now been together for nineteen years."

"But not in the Catholic Church?" I'm remembering what we had been told as children about the sanctity of marriage and the absolute prohibition of divorce.

"We were married as Baptists. I go to the Baptist church—and not even on a regular basis. I don't feel like I'm a Baptist. I still feel that I'm a Catholic. Once a Catholic, et cetera."

"How long have you been divorced?" Rich asks Rose.

"Well let's see. I filed for divorce nine years ago last December. But then my husband fought it tooth and nail. It took me three years and $14,000 to get it."

"Whew," Dave whistles.

"He took it to the state Supreme Court, and he even tried to take it to the United States Supreme Court, but they don't hear marriage cases. So it was just a bizarre situation. But, anyway, he finally found somebody, and they got married. We went through the annulment process, and he was granted an annulment a week before his actual wedding date, which was a year ago last April."

My mind is in a whirl by now. But Dave wants to know whether Rose participated in the annulment process.

"I did. I wasn't protesting his getting married. But I should back up and tell you that I am an administrative assistant to the Senior Auxiliary Bishop of St. Louis. And the metropolitan tribunal, which handles the marriage cases, is in my building. And I did not want these people knowing all my personal ins and outs. So I requested that my bishop get permission to have my marriage case heard outside our diocese. And that's what was done. It was very traumatic—bringing all kinds of stuff up again. I typed fifty pages of documentation in response to all the questions."

"Sheesh," Rich and Dave respond.

"Well, I communicate, and my ex doesn't. I guess that's a woman thing." Rose pauses. "I don't know how I got off on a tangent about all that."

"I've been away from the Church for quite a while," I admit, "and this is a lot different from what I thought as a kid. What you're describing sounds like a Catholic version of divorce."

"Well, yeah," Rich concurs.

"They have a different name for it," Dave says, "because to me an annulment means it never happened. But if you're trying to say the marriage never happened, let's not laugh, because it did."

It turns out that Dave has also been through the process of annulment—at the request of his ex-wife.

"I'm just looking at this thing and going 'Whaa?' So mine was very concise. I just said, 'I agree with my wife.' And sent that baby back."

At this point, I'm thinking that I've been out of touch with the Church, that both Rose and Dave have been divorced, that Dave attends Baptist services, and that Rich has a casual relationship to religious observance. Yet, all of us still think of ourselves as Catholic.

"It sounds like the way we were raised has a lasting influence," I say.

"They drum it into you," Dave comments. "I can see where people say, 'enough is enough,' and they go completely away—or they stick with it 100 percent. But myself, I feel you can still get to heaven and be a good Christian without calling yourself a certain thing."

"Isn't there a quote from Scripture that goes 'When I was a child, I thought as a child, I spoke as a child, but when I became a man . . .'" Rich trails off.

"Right," says Dave.

"And I think I'm still evolving in the process of who God is and what is my relationship to him," Rose offers. "And it can't be based on necessarily everything I was taught in grade school. I think it changes and matures in your lifetime—your growth patterns and your relationship with God. But I think it did—like what you said earlier—it did influence our whole life. Our education at Immaculate Conception, I mean. There was no phase of your life that wasn't touched by the Church."

Rose pauses to catch her breath, and then continues. "Because I didn't have any church support at home. My mother was the Catholic in the marriage, and she was dead since I was three. My father didn't go to any church at all. So the fact that he sent me to a Catholic school, no matter what, I think speaks volumes."

"Says a lot for him," Dave agrees.

"Because I also went to a Catholic high school," Rose continues. "I was the only one in my family of eight children that went to a Catholic grade school and high school. So, I mean, somebody felt it was important."

"Are you the youngest?" Dave asks.

"Yes, well that's another story—but my five children were all raised Catholic and they're all good kids. Though none of them goes to church on a regular basis."

Suddenly we're on different ground—not that of our own religious upbringing, but that of our children.

"My only granddaughter is gonna be six, and my son has

chosen that she's not baptized," Rose says. "My son went to the University of Notre Dame, and yet he's decided that she's going to choose for herself when she gets older."

I'm thinking about my own daughter and the absence of religious instruction in her life. Her father and I were agnostic at the time she was born.

"There's not much you can do about it," Rich says.

"Do you remember being taught that baptism was such an important sacrament that in an emergency anybody could baptize?" Dave intervenes.

"Yes," we respond simultaneously.

"Baptism by blood, water, and desire," Rose muses.

"OK," Dave says, "but were you taught it was only for an emergency? See, I don't remember that it was only in an emergency."

"I remember the emergency part," I say, in a trance of reminiscence. "Even an ordinary person could baptize someone who was dying to prevent them from losing the prospect of eternal life."

"See, my three granddaughters," Dave continues, "I baptized them without their parents' knowledge. Because I firmly believe, you know, original sin, you've got to get rid of that. And I took it upon myself when I was babysitting my granddaughters and the parents went someplace; I took them into the kitchen and put water on their heads."

"It's interesting that you bring this up," Rose says, "because my youngest two daughters and myself, we kind of thought the same thing, that when we had the baby home the first Christmas that one of us would do it. But then we all felt that we didn't have the right."

"My kids don't know it. My brother-in-law does, and you three do. My wife doesn't even know it," Dave confesses.

"I appreciate you sharing this," Rich says.

"Mmmm," Rose muses. "I was really surprised that my daughters felt as strongly as I did about this. But when they talked about doing it also, I thought, 'Wow. We made an impression somewhere along the way.'"

"Well, if my daughters ever decide to have, you know, the girls baptized, I'll just sit back and say nothing. It doesn't hurt to get baptized twice," Dave says. "So, yeah, I feel that strongly about that. As for the part of religion that says you have to go to church on a regular basis, I don't know. To me, if God dwells within you, and you devote your life to him, and you try to do your best in whatever situation you're in, whatever cards fall . . . I mean, everything isn't black and white. . . ."

To rescue us from the perils of theology, I change the subject.

"What is your happiest or most vivid memory of Immaculate Conception?"

"When Lois kissed me on the *Admiral*," Rich says, recalling the annual pleasure-boat ride the whole school took on the Mississippi River in May. "In one of those little picture booths. I don't know if she kissed me or not. Maybe not, I might have kissed her. You know, you put your money in, and you take pictures. I've still got them—unless my wife pitched 'em. I dunno."

"Do you remember school picnics at Chain of Rocks Park?" I say, deep in my own reminiscence.

"We used to go there in buses," Rose says.

"St. Charles Rock Road, west of I-270," Dave adds.

"Yeah, way out there," says Rich.

"I got the crazy idea," Rose blurts out, "in seventh grade, when we wore hoops under our dresses, that for our picnic Lois and Janet Rothenheber and I should all have dresses made— picnic dresses—to wear our hoops. And we all showed up in them at the picnic. You had to go on rides, and they would fly up, which was the stupidest thing. We should have been in shorts or slacks or something. How bizarre!"

For a while we lose ourselves in various school picnics, one of which took place in our own school lot—a full-scale carnival with rented rides. With each resurrected detail from our past, we seem to descend deeper into a space of shared memory.

"I'm gonna tell you something strange," Rich says, at last. "When we were altar boys, we had our sacristy, where we changed our clothes, and then there was the priest's sacristy. There was a big table with flowers piled up. I don't know the names of flowers, but the smell was a good smell, though it was almost overpowering. Remember, Dave? I can still see those green leaves and piles of 'em. It was kind of neat seeing all of those flowers."

"I remember baskets of gladiolas when we sang in the choir for funerals," I say.

"Death flowers, they called them," Rose adds.

"Back then, I had no idea what a gladiola was," Dave interposes. "Flowers were just colors—red, yellow, blue, green."

"I don't know why it jumped into my head," Rich says, almost apologetically.

"Now if I was just sitting down, 90 percent of this stuff, I wouldn't have thought about it," Dave muses.

"You're right," I say, "because when you say that, it kind of surfaces in my own memory, but I would not be able to retrieve it on my own."

"Same here," affirms Rose.

"Isn't it funny how some things stick," Dave says. "I mean I don't remember a lot of that altar-boy stuff, but suddenly it popped up."

"Like Andy Schierhoff," Rich says, "who left to be a missionary—"

"Down in the Andes," Dave says, smiling.

"Yeah," Rich replies. "We made a song on it."

"That we all sang," I say, almost in unison with Rose, "for when he left."

"Down in the Andes with Andy," we begin, a little uncertainly, as if reciting the words of a near-forgotten creed. "Life can be great, can be grandy," gaining speed and assurance with the resurgence of memory. "Things can be fine, fine and dandy. Down in the Andes with Andy!"

And then we sing it again. For the pleasure of being together—and remembering.

Notre-Dame-de-Bon-Secours

> She was the single artificer of the world
> In which she sang. And when she sang, the sea,
> Whatever self it had, became the self
> That was her song, for she was the maker.
> —Wallace Stevens, "The Idea of Order at Key West"

In fall 1996, I fly from Minneapolis to Montreal for a conference on Philosophy and Aesthetics. But I don't fly there directly. When I check my ticket the night before, I discover that Tim, my usually trustworthy travel agent, has sent me to Toronto instead. In a panic, I call his emergency number and plead for help. He apologizes profusely, then finds me a connecting flight from Toronto to Montreal. I will get there in time to deliver my paper.

Even this minor disruption of my plans throws me into confusion. I sleep poorly and feel anxious all the way to the airport. Once safely in the air, I am still feeling disoriented. Yet, I notice with pleasure that the flight is nearly empty; I have a whole row of seats to myself. Slowly, I begin to relax.

Being on the wrong flight, the wrong plane, and on an indirect route to my destination suddenly makes me feel as though I'm in a kind of twilight zone, somewhere outside of ordinary space or time. I sit next to the window, gazing at the clouds below, puffy and white, like a late painting by Georgia O'Keeffe. I'm not that high up—only 30,000 feet—but it feels to me as though I'm in a satellite of some sort, circling the blue marble planet of the earth in a mild and benign orbit.

There is a bank of Skyphones in front of me, and suddenly, I feel an urge to send a message to someone about how free and unmoored I feel, how blissfully lightheaded. I dial the one friend I have who owns a small plane and knows how to fly and talk breathlessly into his voicemail. "I'm on my way to another country," I say, "like that Peter, Paul, and Mary song—'Leaving on a Jet Plane'—and now I'm looking through a misty layer of clouds all the way down to Lake Superior, which is a deep aqua color—so blue, so amazingly blue—you can't imagine."

I'm babbling, but who cares? I'm euphoric. It's like being in love—or looking at the world through the eyes of God.

I've been in love—not often—but frequently enough to make me question my rational self, my carefully constructed life, my ordinary persona. Love has messed me up—disrupted two marriages, leaving me to ponder my solitary condition. The routines of work and friendship seem more reliable. But here I am, up in the air, wondering where I'm going to land, and feeling ecstatic. The difference is that this time I'm my own company. This time, I'm flying high by myself.

I do come down, of course. And go to my meeting and give my paper—something about the traumas in Freud's early life that he failed to grieve. Reading this paper, I am aware of how much my argument owes to my own experience. I've been as evasive—even as ingenious—as Freud in my strategies of avoidance. But now, as a single woman in late-middle age, I feel oddly vulnerable, as if I no longer have any protection against the turbulence of my emotions.

Up until this moment, the only time I can remember feeling integral—as if all the scattered parts of me, like a Jackson Pollock painting cut up and dispersed into fragments, might somehow cohere into a meaningful design—is the last time I fell in love. "Love" being a shorthand for the intensity of this experience. I caught a glimpse of who I might be—or become—and attributed this awareness to the man in whose company I felt such an extraordinary prospect. The result of the ensuing affair was rage from my husband—quickly followed by divorce.

I do not blame him. How could anyone who was not in fact me understand how attached I was to the very imagining of a self that was at once multitudinous and sane?

Indeed, my husband thought I'd gone crazy. Months after our breakup, he confessed to me that my behavior was so out-landish he could only understand it in terms of mental illness. Perhaps if I took Prozac, he offered, I might be cured—or at least return to some semblance of the person I had been, the one he thought he knew and loved.

How could I explain to him that I did not know myself? Yet, as disruptive as my actions had been, they were leading me to something I had to explore. I tried apologizing to him while holding onto some notion of the self I had caught sight of, however briefly, in my affair. He would have none of it.

And now my lover had departed also—impatient with my ambivalence, with the sheer challenge of me.

❧❦

Earlier this year, sometime around the beginning of March, I found myself in Dinkytown, a student-oriented area of shops and restaurants adjacent to the University of Minnesota. The weather was lousy—blustery, snow-packed, and cold. Not just wintry, but deep, sub-zero cold. The kind of weather in which drunks or homeless people freeze on the street. Hypo-thermic cold.

I fought my way from my car to Lundeen's, an offbeat yet upscale jewelry store, where I hoped to find someone to restring a 1920s beaded necklace. Once inside, while waiting for an attendant to emerge from the back room, I examined the merchandise.

There were lots of unset gems in brilliantly lit cases. I bent over them in concentration. One caught my eye. It was a strong orange color, radiating light in all directions. How like the sun, I thought, at this dark moment of the year, in this dark climate. I wanted it. I wanted a small sun I could carry with me—an inexhaustible source of energy to wear on my hand.

Returning to pick up my restrung necklace, I asked the jeweler if I could look at the strange gold stone up close. "What is it?" I asked. "The color is so unusual."

"A sapphire," he said.

"But aren't sapphires blue or violet?" I was thinking of my mother's engagement ring, a lavender oval with a six-pointed star in the center that appeared only in a certain light. I used to ask her to turn her hand until I could see it.

"It's a mineral," he explained patiently. "They come in many colors."

I chose a gold solitaire setting and wrote out a check. As soon as the band was ready the ring would be mine.

Winter would not give up. It was one of those years when it continued to snow well into March. We had a blizzard on the equinox. Nearly a foot of snow piled up, as if it were early December instead of the cusp of spring. But I had my orange-gold sapphire to gaze into.

One night, I had an oddly comforting dream. Though it felt vaporous on waking, I tried to capture it in my journal. This is what I wrote:

> I am extending myself outwards in several directions—like sunrays in a child's drawing. But there's no substance, nothing solid at the core. So I am radiating outwards from this absent center, and this feels disorienting. Yet there may be a circumference. This is not solid either, but rather like the phantom rim of a wheel.

I forgot this dream as soon as I wrote it down. It survives only in the form of my journal entry.

I am a quirky dreamer. Sometimes, for weeks, I remember nothing of my dream life. And then, suddenly, I will have a highly detailed narrative dream—or a simple image, like the radiant light dream that I happened on while spot reading my journal. But if you don't remember something, is it real? And if your only memory is a transcription you hardly recall writing, what significance does it have?

My ordinary life is uneventful. I wake up, stumble downstairs for coffee, where I turn on the radio for company, then crawl back to bed until I begin to feel alert. Sometimes I'll have a second cup of coffee while reading—a guilty pleasure. Then I face the day. I shower, dress, retrieve the paper from the front porch, and fix a bowl of cereal. I check my list of things to do for the week, linger as long as I can at home, then gather books and papers for the short drive to the university. Depending on the weather, I may have to brush snow or scrape ice off my car first. I teach my classes, go to meetings, grade papers, and answer my email. When I come home at night, I change into jeans; eat something simple, like cottage cheese, steamed vegetables, and an occasional pan-fried burger or chop; then read some more; and finally climb into bed, where I continue to read, this time indulging myself with a bowl of frozen yogurt.

Of course, I also go out to dinner with friends, to the movies, parties, art openings, concerts, and theater. My schedule is full, though not remarkable in any way I can think of. My life is not what you would call—by any stretch of the imagination—dramatic.

❧

In 1996, the year following my divorce and the collapse of my affair, I am depressed. Perhaps this explains why winter never seems to end, why my orange sapphire is the only spot of color in my field of vision as the days gradually brighten and lengthen.

Suddenly it is near Easter. One day, on impulse, I accept the invitation of a friend to attend Mass at the monastery of Franciscan nuns she has talked about.

"On Palm Sunday," she says, "it's a bit festive. We gather early in the hospitality room for prayers and songs and then sashay into the chapel with our palms."

I remember Palm Sunday from my childhood at Immaculate Conception Church, but I can't imagine what she means by "sashaying." We were always so orderly, marshaled by the nuns into neat rows and lines. But I've been feeling spiritually desiccated lately, as if I'd hiked out onto a salt flat in the noonday heat. I'm willing to give this a try.

I am struck by two things at the monastery: how warmly everyone greets me and the atmosphere of deep quiet. We do sing and pray before receiving our palms and winding our way through various corridors into the chapel, but the main thing I notice is how many pauses there are in the service—how often we are called upon to listen inwardly. I'm not used to sitting in silence with so many other people. The only analogue I have is a brief foray I made in college into a Quaker meeting. I went there because I liked sitting in a group, not saying anything—a pleasant alternative to going to class or writing papers. I like sitting here peacefully, standing for prayers and responses, but otherwise not speaking. Here I am in a space of solitude that is communal—a space where new thoughts, like small bird flutters, begin to rustle and stir.

At first, I am startled by childhood memories—recalling the palm frond I used to receive at Immaculate Conception Church and carry home to place at the back of my dresser, where it would curl up and yellow, gathering dust balls over the course of the following year. I didn't dare throw it away because it had been blessed. How did I dispose of it when I got a new one? Did the old blessing gradually wear off?

Slowly, my mind turns in another direction, as I attend to the liturgy. I am hearing the Passion story in its bare narrative outline—a drama as full of harshness and conflict as a Greek tragedy.

A friend betrays an intimate friend and then hangs himself in disgust. Another friend, fearing for his life, betrays the same man. A high-level official, who might have prevented an obvious injustice, does a stupid and cowardly thing instead. The man at the center of this drama, who previously seemed so serenely confident, suddenly panics, wishing he could go back, pleading even, to be rescued from the fate he foresees. No one listens—not even his all-powerful father, who has only to lift a finger to save his son's life. His mother, who is not powerful, must witness her son's suffering and death.

It's an awful story. Hearing it now, as an adult, I'm shocked.

The room I'm in is unusually shaped. It's a soft-colored, brick-faced rectangle with high-placed windows emitting a pale spring light and joined to a smaller room, which I take to be the sanctuary. The walls of the first room curve inward at one end, like half-parentheses. In the middle of the sanctuary stands a glass-topped, hexagonal wooden table, which I take to be the altar. Otherwise, there are few adornments. Some potted green plants, a decoupage image of Christ on the cross on the far wall, and a purple, hand-woven banner that signifies the season of Lent.

When it comes time for Communion, I see that everyone—with no exception—moves forward into the sanctuary, forming two semi-circular rows to each side of the altar. The celebrant, a fifty-something man with a broad Scandinavian face and a clear tenor voice, alternately sings and speaks the liturgy. The group I've joined does the same. For this part of the service—except for The Lord's Prayer, which I'd learned long ago by heart—I remain respectfully silent. Abruptly, I feel called to attention, as voices around me rise in response to the drama of Christ's Passion.

"We remember how you loved us to your death," they sing, "and still we celebrate, for you are with us here. We believe that we will see you when you come in glory, Lord. We remember, we celebrate, we believe."

This is my own story: loss, hopeful reminiscence, and the fantasy of return, if not actual transcendence. Why had I not understood this before? Tears start to seep from the corners of my eyes, making me wish I had a tissue. I wipe my cheeks with my fingers, then cup my hands to receive the piece of soft wheat bread that is placed there by one of the Sisters.

"I am not worthy to receive you," I hear from the assembled congregation. "But only say the word, and I shall be healed."

How I wish. As if the hole in my heart could close, like a leaky valve repairing itself.

Though I am a bad, that is to say fallen-away, Catholic—not only divorced but unshriven since my late teens—I do not hesitate to take Communion. In this quiet place, among these hospitable people, it feels right.

Many times when I come here I cry, though I can never predict when a rush of feeling will overtake me, so I learn to pack Kleenex. I also learn to detect the sounds of others sniffling and to feel comforted by the awareness that I'm not the only one caught off-guard like this. Gradually, I allow myself to relax in this light, airy space, whose ribbed ceiling and slightly curving walls make me think of the hold of a ship. Here I may be rocked by memory and emotion, but I am safe—in a vessel that feels as firm as its materials of construction: wood, brick, and stone.

Sometimes I am moved by story—by the imagination that someone (say Lazarus or Jesus) might actually return from the dead or that we might find consolation in such an unlikely possibility. While other times I am moved by metaphor—by the notion of inspiration, for instance, as a tongue of fire. Slowly, I become aware that I've lucked into a community that will carry me—no questions asked—through the cycle of the seasons, while offering me a ritual to mourn all my losses.

Over time, this becomes the meaning, for me, of my childhood religion. It's not about a divine child or some supernatural person who will redeem me from my history of errors and transgressions, but rather a story of loss that I can understand. It's a story I've lived for most of my life.

୬~ଡ଼

Later in the summer I decide to fly out of my usual orbit—to attend a writer's workshop in Spoleto, Italy. Fortified by my orange sapphire, I think it's time to try something new.

I am slow to make my plane reservations, so when I call my travel service in early June and find my agent Tim unavailable, I talk to someone else, who locates me a ticket to Rome, via New York and Paris, but can't book a ticket for the day I want to come home. She holds my outgoing reservation while searching for a return. Two days later, Tim calls to say he's found me a better set of reservations—with a return on the day I've requested.

"This way," he points out, "you'll eliminate one stop, and won't have to change planes—and airports—in New York. Also, it's easier to connect through Amsterdam than Orly. What's more, you'll arrive at roughly the same time in Rome."

"Gosh, thanks," I say. I had no idea I had to switch from La Guardia to JFK, a piece of information the other agent had tactically omitted. Tim has been "watching over" my reservations, as he says, and found me a better route.

One thought I'd had about flying out of New York was that I could touch base with my daughter Jessica, who lives there. But I didn't have much time between planes, and wouldn't be able to see her anyway, so I don't regret this phantom opportunity. Instead, I am flying directly from Minneapolis to Amsterdam, at the same time of day. As a result, I am launched over the Atlantic at the same time I would have been had I flown from New York. A coincidence with no apparent significance. I make the changes Tim suggests and forget my previous itinerary.

Everything goes smoothly on the day of my departure—except that I begin to feel extraordinarily anxious as we head out over the ocean. I try various self-soothing exercises, reminding myself that I haven't taken a trans-Atlantic flight in several years, that I don't quite know how I'll make my way from Rome to Spoleto, and I'm more than a little worried about the writing workshop I've signed up for. Yet, nothing seems to account for my rising panic. Finally, I resort to mantra. "You're in the hands of God," I say under my breath, until finally I begin to relax. Eventually, I feel calm enough to read and later doze off. By the time I arrive in Amsterdam, my anxiety has so far receded that I have trouble believing it actually occurred. A strange episode that makes no sense—no more than my invocation of protection at the hands of God.

It takes me most of the day to get to Spoleto—arriving first at Fiumicino and then taking the express into Rome, where I am bewildered by the crowds and train schedules in Italian. It doesn't help that a wheel has broken off my suitcase en route, so that I feel like I'm dragging an anvil. After an hour or so of standing in lines for information, I understand that Spoleto, listed in impossibly tiny print, is a stop on the way to Ancona. By the time I hand my luggage off the train in Spoleto, I am sweaty and glassy-eyed from lack of sleep. But my destination is worth the effort. Gazing upwards, I see a jewel of a town perched on a hill bathed in rose-gold light. As if on cue, a cab driver appears to conduct me through a benign labyrinth of streets to the Istituto Bambin Gesù, the seventeenth-century convent that hosts my workshop, where I will lodge for the next two weeks.

To enter the convent, you must first walk down a high-walled, cobblestone street, ending at a massive wooden door. Next, you find yourself in a small vestibule, faced by an equally solid door, where you pull a bell-cord, announcing your presence. Then a plump, middle-aged nun appears and shows you to the registration desk. Beyond this room, there is yet another enclosure, an open courtyard, framed by cool, round-arched passageways. My room, as spare as a dorm room with its single bed, clothes chest, and reading light, looks out over this beautiful space, giving me a feeling of airy safety. In the soft evening light, slowly turning from magenta to violet, I feel as though I just may have landed in paradise.

The next morning, I wake to the sound of bells tolling the hour. The nuns, I will later learn, rise early for Matins. They pray at regular hours during the day, interspersing their devotions with the more mundane tasks of managing a guest-house. They are few in number and mostly elderly (the welcoming nun being an exception), and this is how they keep themselves going in the modern world of dwindling recruits and unstable finances. For now, their rooms are full of writing workshop students like me and singers who have come to participate in master classes. We hear their bass tones and arias at odd moments during the day, their musical extravagance a counterpoint to the nuns' sober chants.

At breakfast, I fill a bowl with creamy yogurt and fresh figs and pour myself a cup of dark coffee, looking for an open spot at the long, communal table with other newly arrived members of my group. I introduce myself to those on either side of me and eavesdrop on a conversation across the table.

"Have you seen today's paper?" asks a thin, elegantly dressed woman who looks to be in her sixties. She's been up for hours and has already walked into town to buy a copy of the *International Herald Tribune*, without which she cannot begin her day.

"Look," she says, pointing to a large, black headline, "there's been a plane crash over the Atlantic, just out of New York. TWA flight 800. No survivors. Can you imagine?"

This news jolts me awake and into conversation with my seatmates. "How terrible," we say. "What if any of us"—meaning those who have not yet arrived—"was on that plane?" Because my own flight was scheduled at the same time, I decide to call my daughter to reassure her that I'm all right. After breakfast, I walk into town and buy a phone card to use in a public booth. When I reach Jess, she tells me she wasn't worried because she knew my flight did not originate from New York but that my mother called her for reassurance. She, in turn, called my house-sitter in Minneapolis to confirm my itinerary. I ask her to call my mother again to affirm that she has talked to me live, in order to set her anxiety to rest. I want to be sure that the people who most care about me know I am not dead. After this, I stop worrying about home and focus on the workshop.

At first, the crash is all we can talk about. Are we all accounted for? Is anyone missing? One of us has had a near miss. A young woman in her mid-twenties, who arrives a day late, tells us how she misread her ticket and arrived at the airport in Albuquerque twenty-four hours after her plane had departed. She had held a connecting flight through New York to TWA 800. I can't stop looking at her, stunned by the sheer fact of her being among us—almost a ghost, but vibrant and real, the fullness of her ordinary life still secret and folded up in her.

Gradually we settle into routine, gathering for breakfast, then assembling for our workshop, where we write exercises that we read and discuss. Then we break for a leisurely lunch and a free hour, which some of us spend writing, while others explore the town or succumb to dreamless siesta. Later in the day, we drift into groups of four or five for dinner, strolling the streets for an evening of pasta, wine, and conversation. We forget that one of us has still not appeared, a woman who seems to have sent a message—via the workshop organizer's non-English-speaking babysitter—that she arrived safely in Rome. We breathe a collective sigh, assuring ourselves that no one has been lost, lulled into believing we're all blessed.

One blazingly hot afternoon, I wander down to the Duomo, a pretty little cathedral that opens onto a lovely piazza, both of which seem just the right size for this postcard city. Once inside, I find a pew midway between the vestibule and the sanctuary, from which, in soft-filtered light, I regard my surroundings. I feel calm and happy, though I can't say why. Maybe it has to do with the sharp contrast between sun and shade, or the whispered quiet in this cool, vaulted space.

Gradually I become aware of color and form as I begin to focus on a series of remarkable frescoes depicting the life of the Virgin. The series begins with the moment of her awareness of being with child, continues through the birth of her son, and concludes with her death and assumption into heaven. This story covers the walls and ceiling of the sanctuary in such a way that I feel surrounded, even contained, by it—though I am seated at a distance. It's like being inside a child's picture book, a completely sensuous, nonverbal experience. I am so pleased that I want to laugh out loud, though I manage to suppress this impulse. I wish, instead, that I could stay here forever, contemplating the simple stages of Mary's life—like a repeated bedtime story that never loses its power to enchant.

Slowly my eyes come to rest on the scene of the Annunciation, perhaps the most transparently beautiful of them all. In it, Mary calmly receives light rays aimed directly from the right hand of God, while an angel with wings as delicate as those of an insect kneels before her, raising one hand to his breast and extending with the other a branch of white lilies.

Framed by a portico, which reminds me of the cloisters of the convent where I am staying, Mary looks as serene as a novice considering a life of quiet solitude. While partially angled away from the angel—as if she has been startled from reading the book open before her—she is positioned to receive the light rays touching her shoulder, which will also penetrate her womb. Though her eyes are cast down, her hands are raised over her breast, as if to manifest her sudden agitation.

Later she will suffer a mother's worst nightmare, but there is no sign of that here. No suspicion of tragedy mars the still clarity of this moment, in which everything—including the soft Umbrian landscape in the background—seems suspended in newly washed spring air.

The maker of this radiant scene, holding the world of spirit in such delicate tension with the world of flesh, is Fra Filippo

Lippi, a fifteenth-century monk who immortalized his beautiful mistress in the figure of Christ's mother—all of which I discover later. The only thing I know on this brilliant July afternoon is that an artist who lived centuries before me has given me a feeling of incomparable peace and pleasure.

About a week into the workshop, the leaders take us aside to tell us that the woman whose arrival we had been anticipating any moment (the one who had seemed to call from Rome) was actually on flight 800. Her name is Alecia Carlos-Nelson. She was a former TWA flight attendant waiting for a last-minute courtesy seat. As a result, she was not reported among the victims on the first passenger list. Only the persistence of the workshop organizer, who was puzzled by her failure to show up, uncovered this information. To make matters worse, he tells us, she was traveling with her eight-year-old daughter, Twyla.

So we are not all safe. Two of us (counting Twyla) have died—if not ripped apart by the plane's explosion, then drowned in the waters of the Atlantic.

After receiving this news, I begin to remember my original flight plan. For a period of about twenty-four hours, I had held a reservation from JFK to Paris at the same time as TWA 800. Gradually it dawns on me: my agent Tim had switched me from this flight to the one I actually took.

Never have I felt so close to my own possible death, nor so strangely identified with a woman I have never met and her daughter—who was about the same age as I was when my father died. I could be them, I think; they could be me. I feel very disoriented. Perhaps I died with them and am now in some time warp, sci-fi kind of heaven?

When I catch myself thinking such thoughts, I wonder if my second husband might have been right—maybe I am crazy.

For days I am preoccupied with death—and the quirk of my own survival. Until one afternoon when the workshop leaders take us to the local cemetery for a group writing exercise. Our assignment is to imagine a life based on one of the quaint tombstone inscriptions, many of which include small, glass-encased photographs of the deceased.

The other attraction of this burial ground is a fourth-century church, a partially ruined architectural site and the earliest example of Christian worship in this area. This church, listed in all the guidebooks, is called San Salvatore.

Unlike the Duomo, which beckons the visitor into a miniature, blue-and-gold-painted world, this space is bare and unadorned. The wooden pews are rough, the altar merely a board with a crucifix and white linen cloth, supported by sawhorses. There are signs of reconstruction underway (scaffolding and plywood partitions in the nave), yet no one is at work. A single straw broom lies on a raised platform behind the altar, as if laid there casually at the end of the day and then forgotten. For now, there is no activity, no feeling of purpose or necessity. Nothing is happening here except light, which pours down from an octagonal-shaped dome, creating an effect of quiet luminosity. I notice a range of soft color in the stone walls—milky peach with undertones of ochre and even a pale shade of lavender.

Gradually, the chatter of my thoughts subsides as I sit listening to the beat of blood in my chest and throat, the sift of my own breath. Is this what it means to pray? Not in words or supplications, but in a way of being at ease with one's surroundings and with oneself? If so, I am not so much praying as in a state of prayer. Perhaps I have come to Spoleto for this—to be here, to sit silently in this space?

I stay for an hour or so, while others enter and depart. I close my eyes for an indefinable period of time and nearly fall asleep. At one point I feel an overwhelming urge to cry, as if I am a pitcher too full to contain itself. I don't know—or care to locate—the source of this sudden emotion, though there are reasons enough by now. All that is necessary is to allow it to run through me, like a rush of water through an ancient aqueduct.

This grief, personal or impersonal, passes, and still I do not leave. Now I feel that I am keeping watch, a witness by my presence to some momentous reality—perhaps the weight of death in the cemetery outside, the stinging loss of flight 800, or merely the persistent, small buzz of my own life. When, at last, I feel ready to go, I take the spray of flowers I bought from the vendor at the entrance of the cemetery—a couple of purple and white orchids wrapped in cellophane—and place them on the altar.

I try to give words to these experiences—I'm attending a writing workshop after all—but compose only fragments. My first attempt at a poem, titled "Getting There," consists of a series of questions. It begins:

> What got broken?
> The hinge of my sunglasses
> The crystal of my watch
> The wheel of my suitcase
> What did you leave behind?
> My daughter
> My house and all its possessions

It continues:

> Did you arrive at your destination?
> *Si, sicuro*
> And then?
> The news that burst from the sky
> Like a cluster bomb

Trying to get my mind around Twyla's death, I write:

> A first-century gravestone
> In the *museo archeologico* in Assisi reads
> *Epidia Prisca*, age nine
> *Loco precarilo*, meaning her grave plot
> Could be reclaimed at any time
> By the donor.

One hot afternoon, on a group bus trip from Spoleto to Siena, I jot the following in my notebook:

> How did the field of sunflowers look?
> Like rows of first communicants
> And the tightly-packed hay?
> *Giallo.* Like fat jellyrolls
> What did the angel whisper to Mary?
> *Mi amore, mi tesoro, mia vita.*

"Getting There" concludes:

> Light gleams from the hand of God
> Like an open razor blade.

Before I leave Spoleto I take a train to Monteluco, the little mountain where St. Francis once lived in a hut, meditating on his material life and surroundings. His dwelling is not far from the *bosca sacra*, a grove of trees that was special not only to St. Francis but also his predecessors, the Romans and Etruscans. I walk through Francis's cell, marveling at its small dimensions, then into the woods that inspired him. These trees are old, and they look it—with bulbous roots exposed, gnarled, and snaky underfoot. I feel shy walking among them, not wanting to make a false step—as if I'd stumbled into an enchanted grove where a broken twig might bleed or speak.

Everything here is alive, though not human. Never have I felt so alone in the midst of such intense presence. If anything, the collective being of this wood feels more sentient, more enduring, more real than me.

Long after this trip, I remember places more vividly than people: the convent with its sheltered courtyard, the Duomo with its luminous frescos, the spare containment of San Salvatore, the uncanny life of the sacred wood. But on my return to Minneapolis, where I am thrust back into my daily routines, these images begin to fade—like aging Polaroids.

৯৯৬

Later that autumn, on the morning of my departure from Montreal, I take a walk with a friend into the old city. We head off without a map, aiming for the harbor. Our pace is brisk because of the chill air and misting rain. We pass through wide piazzas and narrow cobblestone streets, charting our course by a distant beacon—a stark gray figure at the apex of a building, looking over the water. Is it some kind of sculpture, I wonder, a tribute perhaps to one of the city's founders?

At last we arrive at our destination—a small chapel fronting the harbor, whose beacon's identity is revealed. She is the Virgin Mary, leaning forward, her hands outstretched over the mouth of the river and the ocean into which it flows, her head encircled by an iron halo of stars.

She looks cold up there to me, a figure of lonely supplication.

We push through heavy wooden doors into a different scene. Here I encounter a warm and delightful little world—more primitive than the Duomo in Spoleto, more cozy than San Salvatore, more human than the sacred wood. There are many paintings, several statues in niches, dozens of burning candles, and, most enchanting of all, hanging lamps in the shape of sailing ships.

A blue light emanates from the dome behind the altar, an aqua shell that seems to represent the sky, with delicate points of silver for stars. The diminutive size of this environment makes me think of a nursery, carefully decorated to entertain a child on waking or to lull it to sleep at night.

This is a church for seafarers and their families. It is a place where people come to pray for those who work on water, their going out, and their safe return. The lead-gray figure on the roof, for whom the church is named, is "Notre-Dame-de-Bon-Secours," Our Lady of Good Help.

Inside, everything is warm and reassuring—a little cosmos made by human hands. Outside, a raw wind whips up the waters of the harbor, a reminder of the ocean's vast unpredictability. The figure on the steeple of the church, leaning into the wind, her arms opened wide, seems distant and frail, but also heroic. What can she do but watch, hope, and endure? She is like Fra Filippo Lippi's Virgin, redeemed from her death but only half-ascended into heaven.

Wallace Stevens imagined a woman who sings to, with, and of the sea—as if giving it a voice through her captivating melody. Yet, the sea is itself and eludes her, so that her words, though calling her listeners to attention, are hers alone. She creates the little world they inhabit together. She is its maker.

And me? Am I like Stevens's enchanted listeners? Or his singer—the sole artificer of my world?

Could there be another possibility? As my kindly therapist once suggested: "You attribute this feeling of cohesion you had in Notre-Dame-de-Bon-Secours to something outside yourself," she said, gently rebuking me in her old-world accent. "But perhaps it is inside you?"

The Wedding Party

Tintern

The unfettered clouds and region of the Heavens,
Tumult and peace, the darkness and the light—
Were all like workings of one mind, the features
Of the same face, blossoms upon one tree;
Characters of the great Apocalypse,
        —William Wordsworth, "The Prelude"

I am anxious about holidays, religious or otherwise. Thanksgiving, Christmas, Easter, Memorial Day, the Fourth of July,
even Labor Day and Halloween. Not to mention birthdays
and other significant anniversaries. No sooner have I gotten
through one cycle than it starts all over again, stirring up
memories I don't especially want to revive. The present can't
help but resonate with the past, yet for most of my adult life
I have reacted badly to this awareness—as if reminiscence
were solely elegiac. A bell tolling for everyone and everything
I've ever lost.

But the eve of the millennium feels different.
    For one thing, it is a unique event, not just because it is
the turn of the century, but because it marks the end of two
thousand years of recorded history. Never mind that the

Gregorian calendar, like every other method of marking time, is arbitrary. On December 31, 1999, the whole world will suspend its breath for a pure, heart-stopped moment of uncertainty—waiting for the universe, like Leviathan, to flash its shining tail before rolling back over again into the deep.

What might happen in this flicker of an instant?

Suppose all computer systems fail at once? Suppose terrorists seize this opportunity to launch a major attack? Suppose aliens land, graves break open, or the moon rains blood? Depending on how you look at it, Y2K could mean the dawn of a new age or the end of everything—the terrible beginning of earth's last days.

On the cusp of this moment, I fly to England to spend an old-world Christmas with my daughter, Jess, and her boyfriend, Jim, at his mother's place on the banks of the Wye, the sinuous, swift-running river that divides England from Wales.

"You can see Tintern Abbey from a hill above the house," Jess had said excitedly on the phone from the UK the year before.

How curious, I thought. I'd read about the Wye and Tintern Abbey—in the poetry of Wordsworth—but had never been there. It was as if my daughter had walked onto a stage set of my imagination.

But for her it was immediate and present. It was real.

I arrive in London a day before Jess and Jim, using the time to catch up on sleep and take a long walk through Regent's Park. The weather, blustery and atmospheric—with heavy clouds and sheets of rain alternately obscuring and revealing the sun—makes me think of Michelangelo Antonioni's movie, *Blow-Up*, with its somber landscape and feeling of watchful presence. Struggling with my fold-up umbrella, I walk until dusk, entranced by the racing clouds and changing light.

The next day, I return to the airport to meet Jess and Jim, who are arriving from New York. Together, we board a bus to

Bristol, where Jim's mother, Di, will pick us up for the final leg of the journey to Brockweir, the village downstream from Tintern, where she lives.

It is storming again when we arrive. Di says there's been rain and high water for some time. "In the village," she tells us, "some houses were flooded on the first floor, though thank goodness the high water mark has passed, and the river has started to recede."

Di, a woman my age and height—but fair-skinned, blonde-haired, and blue-eyed, whereas I am a salt-and-pepper brunette—is dressed practically in a rain slicker and Wellingtons, the ubiquitous rubber boots the English have cleverly devised for tromping in the garden or any kind of muck. She has a no-nonsense attitude toward driving as well, maneuvering her VW stationwagon adeptly through the narrow streets of Bristol and over the bridge spanning the wide estuary of the Severn, which leads to a maze of roads feeding into a series of increasingly smaller lanes as we approach Brockweir.

"It happens quite a lot, you know," she adds, referring to the rise of the Wye and its ritual intrusion into the lives of the villagers, as we make a sharp turn off the main thoroughfare and onto a gravel path leading past a horse stable toward the entrance of her house.

We draw up to a multi-level stone-and-stucco dwelling, the oldest part of which dates to the eighth century. Originally a one-room building with thick walls, low ceilings, and a gigantic hearth, the house gradually expanded, first laterally, then vertically, until it acquired a final two-story addition with high windows looking out over the back garden and a broad, grassy field leading to the edge of the river. A stone wall separates the garden and groomed terrace from the expanse of rough field.

A tangle of black dogs of varying ages and sizes rushes up to the car to greet us. "I'm afraid they're very friendly," Di says. "I do hope you don't mind."

"They follow Mum everywhere," says Jim, petting the largest, least volatile, and presumably oldest of the dogs. "Black labs are very popular here. Most of them she sells, but these five are like family."

"They *are* rather energetic," Di says, turning round to look at me with concern. "I forgot to ask if you have allergies."

"Oh, no," I reassure her, trying to find a head to pat in the mass of moving torsos and legs. Jess has told me about the dogs, but I am surprised by the excitement they stir, their dark shapes a whirl of black intensity in the fading light.

"Would you like a cup of tea?" Di asks, as Jess and Jim, bleary-eyed from travel, retreat upstairs for a hot bath and refreshing nap.

Tea, of course. What better way to ease the awkwardness of a first meeting?

What do we talk about, once we have covered the obvious topics—the weather, travel, London, the house?

Like women in a Jane Austen novel—or the sixty-something mothers of thirty-something children that we are—what we talk about is marriage. Do we believe in it? Is it worth the effort? Can it last? Despite the difference in our cultural backgrounds, Di and I have a surprising amount in common. In late middle age, we are both single women—twice married and twice divorced. We know what is at stake for our children, yet we can't predict their future. During this first evening of our acquaintance—while they bathe or sleep—we discuss the possibilities.

"Marriage is a hazard," I say, "and I haven't done too well at it myself, but I still think it can work."

Di, whose daughter, Lucy, has been separated from her husband for several years, is less sure. "The pressures are so great on families these days," she points out. "I just don't know what makes the most sense."

We are sounding each other out, yet neither of us says the obvious thing. What do we think of our children as potential life partners? The decision is not ours, yet we can't help speculating. The question of their relationship hangs in the air, like the late afternoon mist rising from the river—a ghostly, yet palpable presence.

I sleep peacefully that night under layers of quilts in a snug little room with a gabled window overlooking the garden, feeling like the heroine from one of the children's books I loved—*Heidi*, or Jo in Alcott's *Little Women*. Once, I wake in a pool of milky light emanating from the nearly full moon outside, which draws me out of bed to the window seat, where I peer out at the glowing field and fast-running river in the distance. Both feel familiar in the subdued light, yet also wild and strange.

The next morning, after tea, toast, and marmalade, Di proposes a walk.

"It's a bit steep—and muddy, I'm afraid, at this time of year—but the view is worth it," she says. "And the dogs will get their exercise."

"You'll love it," says Jess. "It's a really old path, leading to a place called Devil's Pulpit. You can see the whole valley from there—Di's house and all the way to the ruins of the abbey across the river."

"You'll need Wellies," adds Jim, "but Mum has plenty. I'm sure we can find a pair to fit you."

Supplied not only with high-topped boots but also thick wool socks to insulate them and a rainproof outer coat with a capacious hood and sleeves that reach to my fingertips (both of which come in handy as mist turns to rain), I set out with Jess, Jim, Di, and all five dogs up a steep incline in back of the house.

The path we follow—though it hardly resembles one in the mud, underbrush, runnels of water flowing downhill, and increasingly dense thicket of trees that spring up around us—has an official, guidebook name. It's called Offa's Dyke Path, Offa being the Anglo-Saxon king who (sometime around 790 AD) ordered a dyke built to separate the lands of Mercia and Wales. Though the dyke is long gone, its trace remains, trodden and re-trodden by centuries of residents and tourists. On the day we hike up, we are the sole travelers. We meet no one coming up or going down—as if we are the only ones who know the way or have the stamina for the climb.

Pretty quickly, I fall to the rear—breathing hard as I work to keep up. Di leads us, closely followed by Jess and Jim, who stride resolutely behind her. The dogs run ahead and then fall back, scouting the trail and herding us like sheep. As the thorns and trees grow up around us and the air thickens with rain, I begin to see us in isolated, almost mythic, terms.

All I can make out are the backs of raincoats, hoods drawn up, moving ahead of me, with the black shapes of animals dashing among them. Once in a while the smallest of these hangs back for a moment and pauses beside me, looking up to see if I am still a part of the group. I keep my eyes on the ground, moving steadily upwards. Surely, there is an end to this trek—someplace where we can rest?

From time to time, I stumble, then recover myself. At one point, Jim reaches over an especially slippery foothold to offer me a hand. I take it as Jess reaches from the opposite side to help pull me up. For a moment, I hold onto both of them, as I locate the next step.

The trail is lined with brambles and slick red branches, the path now obscured by the water flowing ceaselessly downhill. We seem immersed, for a while, in an impenetrable wood. Yet, ahead of me, I can still see Di striding onward, in her dark coat with the dogs swirling around her. Like Artemis, the goddess of the hunt.

I dig my chilled, ungloved hands deeper into my pockets—as if to take hold of some mundane reality. They are filled with random objects: a balled-up linen handkerchief, a couple of smooth stones, some twigs, grains of sand, and a hard, plastic object, which I take to be a miniature flashlight.

All of a sudden, we emerge into a small clearing. We have reached the summit! There isn't much level ground and trees grow thickly even here, but a large outcropping of rock makes for a spectacular view. Jim springs onto it, causing me to draw my breath in a spasm. I've always been afraid of heights and want to stand well back from the edge of anything that resembles a precipice. Somewhat to my dismay, Jess follows him. They stand there, side by side, looking down at the terrain we have crossed. Following their gaze, I can see the whole valley spread out below—the fields descending from Di's house, the river doubled back on itself like a loose brown ribbon, and there, in the distance, the limestone walls and roofless towers of Tintern Abbey.

So, I think to myself, it's not just a poem—but a real place.

I was a graduate student when I first encountered William Wordsworth and the Romantic Movement in literature he helped to inaugurate. I read short poems from the *Lyrical Ballads* (which includes "Tintern Abbey"), longer narrative ones (like "The Recluse" and "The Ruined Cottage"), and even his blank verse epic "The Prelude." Yet, the landscapes Wordsworth described were so foreign to my Midwest-American imagination that I couldn't picture them. They seemed muddy-colored and indistinct, like poor reproductions of famous paintings. Seeing Tintern Abbey with my own eyes is a shock. I now not only want to view it up close, I also want to re-read Wordsworth's poem. Here I am, looking down at the banks of the Wye and the ruined abbey from a few miles above—much as he must have done near the turn of the century two hundred years before. For all I know, he and his sister, Dorothy, even hiked the same trail.

We descend from the promontory by an easier, though slower route—a wide path known as Abbey Mill Road, which served the Cistercian monks until the mid-sixteenth century, when their community was dispersed by Henry VIII, who broke with the Pope to marry Anne Boleyn and head his own church. Every step we take seems saturated with history—like the last stretch of field we cross, swollen with water running down from the hills or rising up from the banks of the river.

We arrive back at the house with wind-chapped hands and cheeks and serious appetites—which Di gratifies with mugs of hot tea, thick sandwiches, sliced apples, cracked walnuts, and ample servings of Stilton cheese shaved from a huge wheel. For this hearty fare, we gather in the oldest (and coziest) room of the house, warmed at one end by a blazing fire in the hearth and at the other by a massive red stove that radiates enough heat to dry a stack of clean towels neatly folded on its covered top.

Pleasantly drowsy afterwards, I wander into the sitting room library in search of something to read—hopefully an anthology of British poetry that includes a sampling of Wordsworth. This room, low ceilinged like the kitchen and dining room, with deep-set windows and wide-planked floors, has a smaller hearth (though there is no fire set in it), a soft couch, and several comfortable wing chairs. I browse the bookcases at the far end of the room, filled with an enticing collection of leather-bound volumes interspersed with porcelain dishes and figurines. Here are the nineteenth-century greats: George Eliot, Charles Dickens, William Makepeace Thackeray, Thomas Babington Macaulay, the Brontës, and Thomas Carlyle. At last my eyes settle on their desired object—no mere selection, but the full collected poems of Wordsworth. I draw it from the shelf, settle myself on the couch with an afghan over my knees, and begin to read.

"Tintern Abbey" is an odd poem—a combination of brooding inwardness and restless energy. Its convoluted syntax and abrupt emotional shifts make it hard to follow. Only in the beginning does Wordsworth sketch a recognizable scene: "these waters, rolling from their mountain-springs . . . these steep and lofty cliffs . . . this dark sycamore . . . these plots of cottage-ground . . . these hedge-rows, hardly hedge-rows, little lines / Of sportive wood run wild." Yet, even here he is more interested in his own state of mind, the "thoughts of deep seclusion" to which the landscape gives rise. It's as if he is using the Wye Valley as a place-marker, a reminder of a location that exists purely within, a product of memory and imagination. The abbey for which the valley is famous doesn't even appear in the poem—other than in its title.

Each time I read it, I feel more baffled. Instead of moving forward, the poem seems to circle back on itself, moving into deeper and more obscure corners of Wordsworth's past. The scene in front of his eyes keeps disappearing, to be replaced by reminiscence, until finally he notices Dorothy standing by his side. She, too, seems to vanish as Wordsworth projects himself into the future, making her mind "a mansion for all lovely forms . . . a dwelling place / For all sweet sounds and harmonies"—turning her into a museum to house his treasured memories.

What to make of this? I'd been hoping for some kind of illumination—a sign or prognostication on the eve of the millennium. But no such luck. After several attempts to plot the poem's strange trajectory, I give up. Another time, I think, closing the book in frustration.

On Christmas Eve we are joined by Jim's Aunt Maria (his father's sister) and her husband, Mike, who accompany us to Midnight Mass at the Church of St. Mary the Virgin in the neighboring village of St. Briavels. Careening through the pitch dark, down one-lane roads bordered by thick hedgerows (where the only way to avoid a head-on collision is for one car to back up to a turnout to allow the other one to pass), I wonder if it might be wiser to say a silent prayer and make an early night of it in Brockweir.

St. Mary the Virgin—as distinguished from the Virgin Mary, I wonder?—looms suddenly before us, its modest limestone façade and tower magnified by the lateness of the hour and the solemnity of the occasion.

"That's a medieval castle across the road," Jim points out, as Di cuts the engine, and we scramble out of the car. I look over my shoulder at a primitive shape, its rounded entryway an arc of blackness, thinking perhaps I should pinch myself to make sure I'm awake. What am I doing here, now, in England?

We're late, so we hurry down the stone pathway—bordered by gravestones lurching every which way out of the ground—into the festooned and lighted church, where the vicar is winding down his homily. We slip, as unobtrusively as we can, into two pews toward the back.

The service, which has evolved from the Roman Catholic one I knew as a child, feels familiar. I am able to follow it by watching out of the corner of my eye for signs of when to kneel, sit, or stand. I even pick up a hymnal and sing—or mouth the words, at least, since I can't really carry a tune—until we reach the turning-point moment: Communion. When this crux arrives, I decide to follow Di, Jim, and Maria to the front of the chapel to accept the thin wafer placed in my hands. Jess and Mike stay behind.

Though I haven't attended Midnight Mass in years (more than I can remember), it feels appropriate. Ritual can help to bind a group—family and not family—in a comforting way. Jim, I notice from the corner of my eye, tears up slightly as we stand for "Hark the Herald Angels Sing," gingerly supporting the hymnal between us.

The next morning, I sleep in—waking in a leisurely way and soaking in the deep tub in the adjacent bathroom before descending for breakfast. Di, an early riser, is already up and out; she and Maria decided to attend a Christmas morning service at the tiny Moravian church a few hundred yards down the road. This church, I learn later (so small as to remind me of a doll's house) was founded in the 1830s on a former cock-fighting site by a high-minded Eastern-European minister. Evidently Brockweir was once populated by sailors, gamblers, and others of ill repute.

Slowly, our little party assembles in the kitchen around the red stove, which is already sending up a delicious aroma from the turkey roasting within. Though I'm not the first to be up and dressed, I'm not the last either. Jess and Jim, the lazy, jet-lagged ones, come downstairs just as Di and Maria return, shedding boots, gloves, hats, and scarves. Mike, who has found a comfortable corner near the giant hearth to read the newspaper, gets up to greet them.

Just then, a green-yellow-and-red-feathered parrot in a cage suspended near the dining area sets up a commotion.

"Don't try to be nice to him," Di warns in my direction as she kisses Mike lightly on both cheeks. "He'll peck you."

"He's a mean bastard," Jim says affectionately. "Always has been."

"He's quirky," Jess adds, "but sensitive. When Di was away once, visiting a friend in hospital who was in a coma, he knew immediately that something was different when she got home. He was making an awful racket—and just that night her friend began to wake up."

"It's a true story," Maria says, bestowing kisses on everyone. "Some things you can't explain."

"Just so," Mike comments under his breath, "but mind that you don't get your fingers near his cage."

"Jim's afraid of him," says Jess. "He got loose once when Jim was little and chased him around, saying awful, dirty things."

"Bloody right," Jim concurs. "I told you he was mean."

This makes me laugh—as the contrast between Jim, who is a rangy and muscular 6'4", and the parrot is extreme. Yet, I can imagine a toddler being terrified of such a voluble and feisty bird.

Cradling mugs of steaming tea, we amble into the sitting room, where Jim has laid a fire in the hearth, each of us donning a festive, tissue-paper crown. These, supplied by Mike and Maria, have a red-plaid design, in honor (I suppose) of some distant Scottish ancestor. Under a small fir tree hung with delicate glass ornaments lie all our brightly wrapped gifts. We open them one by one—as at a birthday party— remarking each one's special virtue before handing it 'round for general admiration. At last, when all have been exclaimed over, including the smallest of stocking stuffers—the chocolate kisses, pop-out eyeglasses, mechanical frog, King Kong, and fire-spitting nun (the last two being my contribution)— we move back into the dining room.

There, we gorge ourselves on turkey with two kinds of stuffing, carrots, Brussels sprouts, whipped potatoes, cranberry sauce, Christmas pudding with brandy butter, individually baked mincemeat tarts, and—as if that weren't enough—Stilton cheese, fruit, and nuts.

Though not precisely in Wales—given that Di's house lies on the eastern (that is to say English) bank of the Wye—I feel as though I have landed in a scene out of Dylan Thomas's magical childhood. Each of us in this small party grouped around the table with our silly crowns, the dogs sleeping contentedly by the fire, the parrot silently observing us from his perch, and the mild winter light filtered through the chintz-draped windows overlooking the garden, the terrace, and the stiff-grassed fields bordering the high-running river—all seem momentarily suspended, as if time has decided not to stop but to idle for a while, before resuming its onward rush.

We stir. We open our party favors and read our fortunes (none of which I remember). We pose for photographs. We discuss politics—Clinton and Monica Lewinsky, the Blair government. We yawn and stretch. We scrape, stack, and wash dishes.

How to occupy the waning afternoon hours? Mike decides on a nap while the rest of us opt for a walk.

Once again, we suit up—choosing from the array of coats, mittens, boots, and scarves in the entryway—then set out for the river path leading past Brockweir in the direction of the abbey. The challenge this time is not the steepness of the route but its waterlogged condition. We choose our steps carefully, looking down first to avoid sinking to our ankles in mud. As before, Di takes the lead, setting a brisk pace with Maria and the dogs, glancing back at us from time to time to see how we are doing. She and Maria, judging from the puffs of cloudy air circling between them, are absorbed in conversation. They pause as we climb, one by one, over a stile in the field, then forge ahead. Surprisingly, they stop at the bridge crossing the Wye to Tintern and turn back toward the house.

"Do you want to go on?" Jim asks. "The path to the abbey is a bit easier, and we can take the road back—or you can catch up with Mum and Maria if you like. It's rather frosty, and Jess says you have trouble keeping your hands warm."

I look at Jess, whose cheeks are glowing and whose fists are dug deep into her pockets.

"Come on, Mom," she urges. "We're almost there. It's beautiful—especially in this light. And we'll be back by tea, I promise."

The mention of tea—from my coffee-drinking daughter—amuses me so much that I agree.

"OK," I say. "I'm not that cold," which isn't exactly true. "And I'd love to see the abbey up close," which is.

We arrive at the ruin near dusk, with just enough low sun to illumine its skeletal limestone form rising up from the banks of the Wye, whose flooded brown waters lie trapped within its low walls like a diluvian phantom—a precipitate of the river itself.

The hour is late, and everything is closed for the holiday. We peer for a while through locked gates, discussing how or whether to climb over them—Jim's idea—before turning back toward Brockweir in the gathering dark.

The sun's descent increases my sense of urgency. Whereas earlier I'd felt a lull in time's meandering flow, now suddenly everything seems speeded up. Perhaps we are all feeling the call of home, as we walk briskly along the road through Tintern toward Di's warm, lighted house.

At first, we walk abreast, Jim's long stride setting the pace. Gradually, however, I begin to lose his rhythm, falling imperceptibly behind. Because the road is narrow and the shoulder virtually nonexistent, this seems natural. It isn't wise for pedestrians to take up too much room on a winding, two-lane thoroughfare. But the distance between us keeps increasing, until suddenly I realize that no matter how fast I walk I will not be able to catch up.

I have a momentary qualm: what if I keep falling farther and farther behind? At almost the same instant I realize that I can't get lost—as long as I can perceive their dark silhouettes, moving steadily ahead.

For a moment, I concentrate on this comforting thought, which then gives way to another startled realization: it doesn't matter. They are walking into their future, absorbed in it and each other. The two, fast-moving figures, so oblivious of me and intent on getting somewhere on their own, are a visual premonition. Of my own place in time—and of things to come.

The day after Christmas in England is called Boxing Day, which doesn't refer to some ancient fighting ritual as I had imagined, but to the custom of boxing food, clothing, and other items for charity. Either that or visiting one's friends to distribute gifts. No one is quite sure when I ask, but these seem the most plausible explanations. In any case, Boxing Day is an excuse to take it easy after the flurry of holiday preparations— or to get out and move around. Di plans on attending the annual hunt, a full fox and hounds affair. Mike and Maria make their departure, as they have other relatives to visit— besides which, Maria pities the fox. Jess accompanies Di, while Jim takes a day trip to visit his paternal grandfather.

Though intrigued by the possibility of a real English hunt, I opt for a small driving trip instead—with a Welsh poet named Gillian Clarke whom I met at a reading in the US and have kept up with by email. Though well known in the British Isles, Gillian has a small following in the States, and I am just beginning to read her. Luckily for me, she and her husband are on their way to visit friends in the area and can easily drop by Brockweir for a half-day tour.

Our first stop is Tintern Abbey.

Though still flooded and closed to tourists, the abbey is at least visible in the full light of day. Before me lies a scattering of low stone foundations; early Gothic portals with delicate tracery; beautiful two-story walls with evenly spaced, arched windows; and a few stately abutments. Well preserved by most standards, the thirteenth-century church and ruins of its earlier buildings nonetheless seem highly impermanent. The overall scene makes me think of the bombed-out cathedrals of World War II, though I know better. To judge by the modern scaffolding on the tallest side of the building, efforts are being made to preserve and stabilize it for future generations. Yet, the standing brown water within makes me wonder. How much can—or will—the Wye reclaim?

"It's kind of eerie, don't you think?" I say to Gillian, as we stand with our backs to the Wye, posing for a photograph taken by her husband, David.

"Right," she says. "You can't help thinking of Wordsworth, can you?"

"But he really didn't write about this—I mean what we're looking at."

"No, he was—shall we say—preoccupied?" Gillian pauses, pursing her lips.

"Come on, love," says David. "Give us a smile."

We turn to face David, who pushes the button on my little Olympus, capturing this fleeting moment—me in my bulky down coat, borrowed from Di's abundant store of all-weather gear, and Gillian in her black wool jacket, white scarf, and shoulder-length, silver-blonde hair.

There's a stone wall behind us, protecting us from the muddy river swirling in the mid-distance, and slabs of slate beneath our feet. If you look at us in snapshot, it's the background that stands out—the far bank of the river, the water below, the wall, the slate—like geological layers of time against which we pose like flimsy paper cut-outs.

Leaving Tintern, we take a leisurely drive north, stopping at several smaller abandoned church sites with towering yew trees and neglected graveyards—heavy stones pushed up and leaning sideways, as if their owners are half-trying to escape, their names, along with their brief histories, long since effaced.

For lunch, we stop at the Skerrit Inn, the oldest (so its sign says) in Wales. In a warm, dark-paneled room, we pursue our discussion of Wordsworth over sausages and ale.

"I don't get it," I confess to Gillian. "'Tintern Abbey' has no structure—it doesn't really make sense."

"Well no," says Gillian. "I agree with you on that. But if you look at it in terms of isolated passages or flashes of insight, it takes a different aspect. Mind you, I'm not much for Wordsworth."

"Me neither," says David, who is an architect and clearly grounded in the materials of his craft. "But Gilly's right. Don't look for structural cohesion but for something else—something like breakthrough moments?"

"He kept trying to get to something," Gillian adds, "and mostly failed, but once in a while, he succeeded. You have to be patient—and wait for that."

"Ah," I say, thinking of Gillian's own poetry—so graphic in its description of day-to-day objects and experiences and close to ordinary reality—unlike that of Wordsworth, who believed in using the language of common people, yet whose diction hardly sounds common.

"There are some beautiful lines," Gillian continues as an afterthought. "Some really astonishing ones."

On the way home, we stop at Hay-on-Wye, a town that seems comprised almost entirely of booksellers; the streets are jammed with shops specializing in all kinds of new, used, and rare volumes. So single-minded is Hay-on-Wye that it seems like a fictional place—a town made of books—like something out of a story by Borges.

"Every year," David says, breaking into my spell, "they host a festival, attended by hordes of people—dealers, publishers, editors, famous writers. A real mob scene." He glances sideways at Gillian, gauging her reaction.

"Gilly's been featured too," he continues. "She says she hates crass publicity, but secretly she loves it."

"Readings galore," says Gillian, sticking her tongue out at David. "It's quite a spectacle—and a good bit of fun. Like a country fair—a mix of everybody and anybody. Do come back, and I'll show you around."

Jostling and joking with each other, we amble down cobblestone streets, peering through dusty windows and occasionally dropping in to browse until the ever-present drizzle turns to rain.

At which point, we make a dash for the car.

We arrive at Di's by late afternoon—after a slow, sinuous descent through a series of hills and valleys, alternately darkened by clouds and illumined by fitful bursts of sun, the dun color of the hedgerows and denuded trees contrasting vividly with the fields' vernal-seeming green.

On my last day in Brockweir, we make a bonfire in the field—something impossible in all but the most remote areas of the States. Jim and Di work steadily from breakfast to noon, gathering and chopping dead wood from various corners of Di's property. Jess helps some, and I come out to photograph while the dogs prance around us all, running off with loose sticks whenever possible. At last, the pyre is ready—but will it light? Everything is so drenched, with the furiously churning Wye a reminder of the recent floods.

"Don't worry," says Jim. "We know how to do this—it's a family tradition."

"You can't have Christmas without a bonfire," adds Di. "And it's so practical. I count on James to help clear the field."

"In the summer," says Jess, "Jim has a party out here—a kind of midsummer fling. People come dressed in all kinds of costumes."

The pile of wood and branches smoke at first, then suddenly break into flames, which rise quickly and brilliantly. Sparks fly up like Fourth of July fireworks, arcing into the cool, already darkening air before sinking back into the wet earth. Heat fans my cheeks and warms my hands as I stretch them before me, palms open to the flames. Jess stands beside me, as mesmerized as I by the sudden spectacle of light.

Jim and Di busy themselves tending the edges of the fire, occasionally feeding a new branch to its incandescent heart. The bonfire holds us all in its hot embrace—until it begins to sigh, collapsing slowly into itself. At last, all that remains is a bed of coals, flashing and glowing, like a cluster of will-o'-the-wisps on a summer's night.

As Jim rakes the remains into the wet ground, the rest of us—including all five dogs still leaping and playing in the wide-open field—turn reluctantly back to the house.

I don't stay for New Year's. Di doesn't celebrate this holiday. Jess and Jim are traveling to Scotland, where they plan to ring in the millennium in a Highland castle with friends.

We part in stages. Di drives us, in the frosty, pre-dawn hours, to Bristol, where we embrace and kiss (in the two-cheeked British way that I'm now getting used to) before Jess, Jim, and I board the bus to Heathrow, where we kiss again (in the American body-hug way) before heading to our separate gates. I arrive at mine just in time for my non-stop flight to San Francisco.

A day or so later, I pack my rental car and drive up the coast to Mendocino to join a small gathering of friends in a house overlooking the Pacific. Better here, I think, than an urban center. If anything really does go wrong, I'll be far enough from a big city to be safe.

Around midnight, my friends and I pull ourselves away from our comfortable chairs and the bristling fire in the stone fire-place to walk out onto the damp and cold deck—clasping our glasses of champagne and searching the dark ocean (which we can hear but not see) for clues to our destiny. We listen to the steady, rhythmic push of waves against the shore, raise our glasses in salute, and then scurry back to the warm shelter of the house.

In the morning, we rise, make coffee, shower, and dress. The sky is overcast, gloomy. Low clouds hang over the ocean, permitting only small gleams of sunlight to break through. Nothing has changed: no computers have crashed, the stock market stands firm, the sun shines as usual, and the moon maintains its faithful orbit around the hectic earth.

Late in the morning, I take a walk to a lighthouse on a bluff, where I stand—hood drawn up, hands dug deep into my parka—facing the unruly Pacific. I hold my ground in the wind and mist just long enough to notice the play of light over the churning water. The sky is not uniformly gray—as if obscured by fog. It is a scene of constant movement.

Clouds change position with the swiftness and ease of dancers, causing bursts of sun to flash blindingly and unpredictably on patches of the water below. These shine flat and laser-like, a pure platinum white—like the sun itself, too annihilating to gaze into. Yet, I can't take my eyes from this panorama—shifting, expanding, and contracting, like a sign or summons but one composed entirely of water and light.

All day I watch it. At first from the bluff but later from the deck or through the floor-to-ceiling windows of the house.

Light rides towards the shore, as if preparing a glittering path on which I would not be surprised to see angels descend. Then, just as suddenly, it retreats to a single spot of diamond-like brilliance. Yet, it never disappears entirely. Companion-like, it flashes before my eyes whenever I turn to look.

I'd been preparing myself for something more dramatic. What I get is a light show on a gray day over the Pacific.

There is a surprising truth in ordinariness—much as Wordsworth was taken off-guard and captivated by the least promising of scenes and objects. When he sought a vision or mystical awareness, it eluded him—which may account for the strain I feel in "Tintern Abbey," in which he tries too hard to animate a former state of bliss. But when he lets go of anticipation, something new leaps forth that is wild and strange. At one point in "The Prelude," he refers to this condition as "visionary dreariness," a phrase that had no meaning for me as a graduate student—believing that life should offer more positive excitement.

But now I wonder.

What if life coheres for us randomly and unexpectedly—in

moments of pure concentration—like the sun mirroring itself on the Pacific?

What if this is the message we have been waiting for, yet turn away from, uncomprehending?

When Other Worlds Invite Us

Whenever other worlds invite us, whenever we are
balancing on the boundaries of our limited human
condition . . . that's where life starts.
—Philippe Petit

I wake up ragged from a night of bad sleep. No surprise about that, as I have a class to teach at noon and tend to obsess about my lectures. Yet, it is the second week of the semester, when normally I feel less anxious. I keep telling myself this as I try to follow my usual routines, restless and unable to concentrate.

I'm about to check my email when the phone shrills, making me jump.

"It's Jim," a British-inflected voice breaks in. "I'm calling . . . to let you know there's been an attack on New York, but Jessica is all right."

"What?" I say, trying to adjust to the fact that my daughter's fiancé is calling me, when most of the time I call one of them first.

"It's . . . it's Jim," he says again with the slight stutter that occasionally interrupts his speech.

"Oh, yes!" I reply, not wanting him to think I don't understand. I sometimes have trouble with his accent and feel embarrassed about this.

"It's just . . . that there's been this attack on the World Trade Center, but I want you to know that Jess is safe."

"Uh-huh," I say, searching for some context for what Jim is saying. Wasn't there a bombing of the World Trade Center in the early '90s? A truck or something in the garage?

"And she's seven blocks away," Jim continues, "so she's . . . she's all right."

"Oh, good. I'm so glad to hear that."

"Right," Jim says, adding apologetically. "These things happen, you know, in New York."

"Ah," I reply, feeling rueful about the level of violence in my country.

"Just wanted you to know."

"Thank you for calling," I say, not fully absorbing what Jim has said. "I really appreciate it."

Foolishly, I hang up.

The next thing I do is turn on the TV, where rapid-fire images assail me. Planes flying into glass towers, spectators pointing upward, clouds of debris chasing people down the street, TV anchors struggling to keep their voices even, panic in their eyes. The South Tower is already gone. Billowing fire and ash, it has come down in ten seconds flat.

Before my eyes, the North Tower crumbles. I watch as it collapses, tier upon tier, all the way to the ground. Even in my stunned state, I marvel at how quickly it gives up the ghost, falling like a plumb line—as elegantly as a building designed for demolition and as flimsy as a wedding cake.

I stare at the spume of vaporized steel, glass, and concrete. Seven blocks is nothing. From what I can see, all of lower Manhattan is enveloped in smoke, covered with ash, or burning. I picture Jess on the street in the midst of this hellish scene—running.

"I'm with you," I say, bursting into tears. "I'm your mother."

Only a month before, Jess had called to announce her engagement. Though I'd been hoping for this, I'd also tried to keep my fantasies to myself. Yet, I'd already begun to think of her together with Jim, having a family. When they moved into a spacious apartment in Brooklyn, I gave them some china and crystal my mother had left to me, thinking they had a broader social life than I and would make better use of it.

But where is she now? What was she doing in the city when she normally works from home in Brooklyn? Why didn't I think to ask?

I pick up the phone. I don't try Jim, as I assume he was calling from work in Manhattan—at a firm whose name I stupidly can't remember. And I don't call their apartment, since I know Jess isn't there. If I have any hope of reaching her, it is by cell. Over and over I dial, waiting for the buzz, the "we're sorry, this call cannot be connected," then punching in the numbers again. "Please, please, please," I mutter, my eyes fixed on the TV—as if it were some kind of oracle.

Who else can I call? I try my ex-husband, Frank. We've been divorced for over twenty-five years, but I want to talk to someone who might understand how I feel. No answer. I leave a message that goes something like this: "I'm sure you've heard about the disaster in New York. Call me."

For about an hour, I am alone with my portable phone and TV.

Then, suddenly, I hear a ring on the other end—before the line clicks off. Thank God for technology, I think. If her cell can ring, she must be alive.

Before I have time to dial again, my own phone springs to life.

"Mom," I hear on the other end. "It's Jess."

Scarcely a week after the World Trade disaster, Jess and Jim come to visit me in Minneapolis—a trip we'd planned long before 9/11. Though regular flights have resumed, everyone is still nervous. Since the attack, I've been viewing the skies with suspicion. When I detect a plane, my first thought is "who is that and what are they doing up there?" I have to remind myself that seeing an airplane in the sky is a sign that things have returned to normal.

The day that Jess and Jim are to arrive, Jess calls me at home to say they'll be delayed. There has been a bomb scare at JFK. The entire terminal is emptying onto the sidewalk as they drive up. They're on their way to LaGuardia to find another flight.

"It's scary," she says before they get on the plane, "but they didn't find anything. It was either a hoax or a false alarm." She gives me the new flight information.

I drive to the airport, prepared for the fact that I won't be able to meet them at the gate due to heightened security. I arrive early and go to the baggage claim area to wait.

And wait.

Each time a new group of passengers appears at the top of the stairs, I scan their faces expectantly. Slowly they disperse, with no Jess or Jim in sight. According to the monitor, their plane has landed. But as the minutes stretch into a quarter of an hour, then half an hour, then a full hour, I become increasingly anxious.

I re-check the baggage claim monitor, but the flight information I'd seen earlier has vanished. What has happened to Jess's flight? Has it disappeared into thin air?

I don't want to leave the baggage claim in case they arrive in my absence, but my fear is now out of control. What if something has happened to their plane in mid-flight and the airline is covering for it? Suppose their flight has been diverted somewhere and crashed?

I abandon my post to find an airline representative.

"It shows here that the plane is on the ground," the woman at the ticket counter says, her polished nails clicking on the keyboard of her computer, "and there's only one exit from the security area, so I suggest you go back and wait."

I rush back downstairs, only partly reassured. Nothing has changed. No Jess; no Jim. I begin to talk to strangers.

"Which flight are you waiting for?" I say. "Oh, un-huh, well I've been waiting for over an hour and am just wondering if you know anything about the flight my daughter is on from New York. Yes, well this whole thing is a little nervous-making, isn't it?"

After another twenty minutes, I go back upstairs, desperate for any kind of information. This time I get a different story.

"Well it seems that the plane from New York is on the ground," the agent says, "but there's been a security breach at the airport, and no one can deplane."

"What kind of security breach?"

"Someone ran through the checkpoint," she says coolly, "and that concourse has been closed until they find him."

This information is not comforting. Is there some kind of terrorist loose in the airport?

"I'm sorry I can't help you more," the agent says. "You'll just have to wait."

In the next half hour, I relive my anxiety of the week before. "Please, please, please," I murmur under my breath. "Let them arrive. Let them be safe."

Two hours after their scheduled arrival time, I see Jess and Jim descend the staircase to the baggage area, where I've been numbly waiting.

"We got here on time," Jess explains, "but we've been stuck on the plane until now. They wouldn't tell us why. I left a message at home for you but didn't know how else to reach you."

"You know what?" I say, hugging and kissing them both. "It's time for me to get a cell phone."

Under the best of circumstances, Jess is phobic about flying. We've talked about this often.

"I don't know," she says. "It's OK when I get on, and even when we take off, but then, sometime when we're up in the air—really high, you know, like 30,000 feet—I begin to worry about what's holding us up."

This is a question I can't answer—though to tell the truth

I haven't ever thought to ask. My anxieties tend to focus elsewhere—on making reservations, getting to the airport on time, or what to do when I arrive at my destination. It's the transitions that worry me, not the flight itself.

When Jess was in high school, I asked my physicist husband to explain to her how airplanes fly, hoping that his clear, rational manner would reassure her. But it didn't take.

Then I began to worry that I was at fault. Perhaps the years when she traveled as an unaccompanied child between me and her dad, in our various geographic relocations, had taken an insidious toll.

Before 9/11, I had tried to downplay the danger of flying—in part because I didn't like to think about how I might have contributed to Jess's fear but also because I thought it was genuinely unfounded.

Now I begin to share her anxiety.

The first trip I take after 9/11—to a meeting in Washington DC—is scarcely a month later. Because I've planned it long in advance and know I'll have to fly sometime, I steel myself to get on the plane.

Aside from the fact that I can't arrive or depart from National Airport (which is closed), everything goes smoothly. Yet, the meeting is sparsely attended, and we can hardly talk about anything else. On the way to and from my hotel, I pass the Pentagon, which I'd never noticed before. Now, suddenly, it's a tourist spectacle. Both of my taxi drivers point to it solemnly, and I can't help staring at its hulk. It lies there, looking oddly vulnerable in mutilated form—like some massive, prehistoric creature that has been bludgeoned by a giant axe.

Yet, I continue to gamble on the skies.

Three weeks later, I fly to Texas, where I join Jess for a visit to her grandmother in Wichita Falls. We've been making this an annual trip—ever since my mother died three years before. Though her dad and I rarely see each other, I've begun to reconnect with his extended Texas family, mainly through his widowed mother, Nellie May, who urges me to come see her, with or without Jess.

Usually we coordinate our schedules and pick a date, then fly to Dallas/Fort Worth, where we rent a car and drive together to Wichita Falls. At the end of our trip, we repeat this pattern in reverse. After three years, we've fallen into a comfortable routine, varied occasionally by the arrival of one of Jess's cousins from Memphis or Los Angeles.

One magical year, we all came at once: Jess and Jim from New York, her cousin Ross from Memphis, Robin from LA, and me from Minneapolis. Jess's Aunt Marilyn drove down from Oklahoma, where she and her husband operate a horse ranch, with her children, Jamie and Lloyd, while her uncle Bob and Aunt Theda, who live in Wichita Falls, brought nightly barbecue for dinner.

This time, it is just Jess and me, though Bob and Theda are frequent visitors, along with other friends and neighbors. It is close to Halloween, and every time someone comes to the front door, a paper owl dangling over the entryway hoots, startling us all and making us laugh.

Nellie May's house is a hub of activity, though she herself is pretty much confined to a wheelchair or recliner during the day and needs round-the-clock assistance in order to continue living at home. In her younger years, she was always on the go, so she takes it hard that she's now so immobile. "If I knew I was going to live so long," she says ruefully, "I'd have taken better care of myself."

Nellie May's father died when she was a teenager and her mother when she herself was raising a family. Now in her eighties, she is surprised by her longevity. "I just wish I could do more," she says. "I feel so useless."

"Nanny, you haven't changed," Jess reassures her. "You've always done so much for us, and now you deserve a rest."

"Your spirit is the same," I add, "and that's what counts."

જ⁊ઉ

I am remembering another, long-ago moment in time, when Nellie May played a dramatic role in my life. In the spring of 1979, Jess went to visit her in Wichita Falls over spring break. Both her dad and I had travel plans that week, and, to avoid quarreling over who would be able to leave town, we agreed to send Jess to Texas to stay with her grandmother. As a result, Frank went to Colorado, where he was teaching a month-long photography workshop, while I made plans to attend a conference in San Francisco.

On the day before my departure, I taught my class, as usual, on campus—where one of my students (who knew about my travel plans) asked if I'd heard about the tornado in Wichita Falls.

"What tornado?" I asked.

"Well, it's all over the TV," she said. "I saw it on a monitor in Coffman Union, and it looks pretty bad. You might want to check with the National Guard or the Red Cross."

I ran to the Union after class to find out what I could—I discovered that three separate funnel clouds had joined to cut a swath a mile wide through the city of Wichita Falls. The sky was black with whirling energy.

Where was Jess?

I ran back to my office to make phone calls—to Nellie May, to the Red Cross, to local radio and TV stations none of which went through. The National Guard gave me some zip code areas that had been affected, but that was all. Then I sped home, where I stayed glued to the TV, trying to gauge which parts of the city had been hit. I called Jess's dad, whom I could not locate at the number he had given me. Then, in desperation, I called the Colorado Springs Police Department to ask if they could find him in an emergency. All day I waited, wondering what had happened to my daughter—and everyone else in her dad's family in Wichita Falls.

Finally, I called my mother. I'd avoided calling her earlier, knowing how easily upset she was, but I'd run out of options. For once, she was surprisingly calm.

"What about her Aunt Marilyn in Oklahoma?" she asked. "Why don't you try her?"

"Brilliant," I said. "I bet she knows something by now. But I can't remember her married name and don't know her number."

"Wait," my mother said, as she began to rifle through her ancient address book—with numbers written in pencil, crossed out and written over, pages falling out. "Here it is," she announced. "I've got a number in Edmond—and her last name is Peters."

"Thanks, Mom," I said, grateful for my mother's archival habits. "I'll call her and get right back."

I hung up, dialed again and got through on the first try. Never have I been so happy to hear a Texas drawl.

"Everyone's aw-right," Marilyn said. "Mother took Robin and Jess out of town to see Dad's sister in Marshall. They weren't even there during the tornado. Dad was at home, but the tornado missed the house. Aunt Margie laid in the bathtub, but her house is OK too, just a few broken windows. And everybody else, Bob and Theda, Aunt Carolyn and Uncle Jug, Elsie and Maurice and their children are all OK. Just a little shook up. Mother called me this morning to let me know and said she'd left a message with Frank. He was supposed to pass it on to y'all."

"I'm so relieved," I said over and over. "I can't tell you how good it is to hear your voice."

I called my mother to let her know that Jess was safe and began to pack for my trip the next morning.

Not long afterwards, I heard from Frank.

"I tried to reach you in the morning," he said, "but there wasn't any answer, and I didn't know your number at the university. I was on a field trip with my students the rest of the day."

"Well, if you get a call from the police, don't be surprised," I said, only half-joking. "They're looking for you."

That evening was the first night of Passover, and I was planning to go to a friend's house for Seder. I had called him earlier to say that I didn't want to leave the house until I had news of Jess. I rang back later to say I'd be there. After a day spent alone with the phone and the TV, I wanted company.

It was a small gathering—just me, my friend, his brother, and his brother's girlfriend. Although we weren't doing everything by the book, I heard clearly the story of Exodus.

"Why is this night unlike every other night?" the service began.

I heard a story that went straight to my heart.

How God helped Moses lead his people out of Egypt—sparing them from plagues of pestilence, frogs, flies, lice, locusts, and rivers of blood. Telling them to mark the doors of their houses, so they'd escape the final scourge on first-born children. How Moses foiled Pharaoh's army by parting the waters of the Red Sea. How Pharaoh's army perished.

I'm not Jewish, but I understood at least one of the meanings of Passover—how it might feel literally to be "passed over." That night was unlike any I could remember—as the Wichita Falls tornado had spared my daughter and her Texas family. No one I loved died that night. Brushed by the wings of a whirlwind, they all survived.

❦

The morning of our departure from Wichita Falls, Jess and I get up early, pack our bags, and visit with Nellie May until it is time to go. We eat breakfast with her in the kitchen and then move to the living room, where Nellie May's caregiver, Joanne, helps her maneuver out of her wheelchair into the more comfortable recliner, while Jess and I settle ourselves on the couch.

All at once, Jess starts talking about 9/11.

Some of what she says I've heard before—when I finally reached her on the phone that day—but I am hearing it differently.

"I was taking the Q train to Manhattan," she says, "to meet with my friend Christie for the first day of a job we were doing together." Christie is a television producer, who worked with Jess on her first independent film. They met as under-graduates in college and have been friends ever since.

"From the train, I could see the towers burning. And I knew what it was." The Q train—though technically a sub-way—crosses the East River above ground, so you can see the lower end of Manhattan.

"So, I got off—and went to the place where Christie and I were supposed to meet." This is the intersection of Jay and Greenwich streets—a mere seven blocks (as Jim had said) from the World Trade Center.

"But nobody was there. And the building was dark, so I walked back out to the street."

Months later, I walked downtown from the office where Jess was then working to this spot. I wanted to know where she had stood and to imagine how she might have felt.

"Suddenly, I heard a terrible rumbling, and the ground was shaking—like an earthquake. I couldn't see the tower, but I knew what must be happening. So, I thought 'I guess I'm going to die.' I wasn't afraid. I felt calm—so I just stood there. If you're going to die, there's nothing to do. But then I saw all of these people running past me, screaming and crying. And I started to run with them."

Jess actually was on the street—as I had pictured her—running.

"But then it was over. And I thought, 'I guess I'm going to live.' My next thought was that I should find a telephone—because my cell phone wasn't working. But everyone was rushing to the public booths. And then I remembered that I have a friend who has an apartment in Tribeca, so I started to walk there."

Jess's voice is even, but her eyes have an inward look. I put my hand on her knee and glance over at Nellie May.

"We were all so worried, thinking about you," Nellie May says, "and we're grateful that you're safe. It's just so good to see you both. I wish—"

Joanne appears in the doorway to the kitchen.

"When did you say your flight was?" she asks. "Maybe y'all better come look at this."

I hear a TV droning in the background.

An American Airlines flight has taken off and crashed at JFK. This is not the same as 9/11, but an airplane is involved, and Jess is about to fly back to New York. I watch as her eyes darken with fear.

Jess calls Jim in New York, while I stay in the kitchen with Joanne, scanning all the networks for the most up-to-date information. Fortunately, we have a couple of hours to decide whether to stay or go. At last, all sources seem to agree that the crash—its cause still unknown—is not a result of terrorism.

When I return to the living room with this news, I notice that Jess is silent and remember how I used to gauge her mood as a child by her chatter. When she was happy, she would overflow with conversation. Even as a two-year-old, she'd talk in a bubbly monologue, as if she couldn't help expressing what was going through her baby mind. But when something bothered her, she would grow quiet.

"It's going to be OK," I say, making an effort to steady my voice. "This isn't another 9/11. Trust me; I'm your mother."

The crash is bad but not part of a wider pattern of terror. This, at least, seems clear by the time that Jess and I drive back to the Dallas/Fort Worth airport. Still, I am reluctant to leave her and make her promise to call me when she arrives in New York. At my own gate on a separate concourse, I scan the TV monitors for breaking news and scrutinize my fellow travelers carefully.

This isn't just a "near miss" story—though it is partly that, like the Wichita Falls tornado. And it isn't only about Jess—as Jim, who normally takes the subway under the World Trade Center to work in lower Manhattan, stayed home that day because (like me) he couldn't sleep the night before. Nor am I suggesting that the people who died are any less special to those who loved them than my daughter and son-in-law are to me. Or that some inscrutable deity was rolling dice that day—decreeing all our fates.

This isn't a story with a moral of that kind. Rather, it's about a feeling I can't quite pin down—like a word on the tip of my tongue, or an image hovering on the edge of my vision. Something ghost-like or uncanny.

It's about the time-lapse quality of my watching the North Tower come down, mirroring the collapse of its twin approximately an hour earlier. As if Jess's experiences were being replayed before my eyes. Or as if clock time had been suspended, causing Eastern and Central Standard Time to fuse with each other. As if time had suddenly collapsed on itself or done a backwards somersault. Time as metaphysical stunt pilot, performing loop-de-loops.

Or a mother-daughter déjà vu.

જ઼ન્ઙ

After hearing from Jess on the morning of 9/11, I call Nellie May in Texas to make sure she knows that Jess is OK.

"I was so worried," I say. "It reminded me of the tornado."

"I know," Nellie May replies in her plainspoken voice. "We were all so lucky then—and now."

Then I hear from Frank.

"I called," I tell him, "because we're Jessica's parents—I needed to talk to you."

"I just got your message," he says. "Jim called earlier, so I knew Jess was all right, but it's pretty hard to take in." He pauses, drawing a breath. "I've been thinking about you too."

I try to explain how time seemed to double back on it-self as I was watching TV, but I know I'm not making sense. Finally, embarrassed about not taking Jim more seriously, I repeat his comment about how "these things happen in New York."

"It's that British understatement," Frank says, chuckling. "Stiff upper lip and all, but he was probably in shock."

"What could he say? That terrorists have attacked the World Trade Center and one of the towers has fallen and Jess is somewhere nearby?"

We are both silent for a moment.

"Remember that tornado?"

"When it was over, it was over," Frank says quietly. "Who knows where this will end?"

I watch TV for a while longer, then rouse myself to go to campus. Classes have been cancelled, but it occurs to me that some of my students may not have gotten the message and will show up, bewildered. Also, I need to see other people. Out of a class of thirty, two arrive—knowing what has happened—and we talk for a while before disbanding.

I spend a couple of hours in my office emailing friends who live in New York, to see if they and their families are all right. Then I go home, where I sit in the blue glare of the TV until a friend calls to ask if I want to come with her to a service at the Basilica. Gratefully, I accept. I am becoming addicted to watching the video replays of the towers falling.

After the candlelight service, I return to my private vigil next to the TV. I watch until I see Peter Jennings on the verge of breakdown—his face sagging, mind scrambled, barely able to complete a sentence or keep himself from crying.

In the days following, I call Jess every day—needing to be assured that she is alive. And I return to the TV whenever possible. Over and over again, I watch the planes—mere flecks on the screen—aim toward the distant towers, slicing into them like flaming swords, the buildings burning like torches. Then the precipitous fall, one after the other, like Siamese twins who cannot bear to be divided.

Several months later, I happen on a PBS special titled "The Center of the World," part of a series on the history of New York, which deals with the World Trade Center—from its conception in the post-war period, through the twenty-year process of its planning and construction, to its zenith in the 1990s, and its nadir on the morning of 9/11.

Here is a clear, sequential narrative. Now, perhaps, I can get my mind around what has happened. Instead, what I focus on—and later remember as the whole episode—is the most ephemeral moment in the buildings' history.

In the late summer of 1974, a young Frenchman, who had been excited by the idea of the twin towers long before they were completed, labored all night to string a steel cable between them and then walk it with only a circus-performer's balance bar to steady him. His name is Philippe Petit, a celebrity at the time but a nearly forgotten figure thirty years later—until the collapse of both of the towers he had so tenuously connected.

This was no daredevil feat. It was carefully planned: first conceived in the heart of a future high-wire artist, nurtured for six years as he perfected his craft, then plotted on site for a full eight months as Petit studied the buildings, getting to know them inside and out, to the point that he felt he had "married them."

On the evening of August 6, he and two accomplices ascended to the rooftop of the South Tower, carrying with them 250 feet of braided steel cable, along with a bow and arrow to arc it—like a fly-fishing line—to the edge of the North Tower. They worked the rest of the night to secure the rigging. Then, around 7:00 a.m. the next morning, Petit stepped out onto the wire—110 stories above the ground and 1,360 feet in the air.

"I was overwhelmed," he says, "by a sense of ease, of simplicity. I knew I was in my element."

Not only was he not fearful, he was "happy, happy, happy."

In the next forty-five minutes, he made no less than eight crossings between the buildings, each one more playful than the last. He would take a bow, bend to one knee, even salute the horizon.

A crowd of spectators gathered on the ground, pointing upward—applauding and calling encouragement.

One of the police officers dispatched to the North Tower to arrest him stood well back from the edge, dumbfounded.

"He was a tightrope dancer," he says, "doing a dancing routine on the high wire. He laid down and just lackadaisically rolled around. He got up and started walking and laughing and dancing, and he turned around and ran back out into the middle. He was bouncing up and down—his feet were actually leaving the wire."

Finally Petit reclined on his back, one leg extended before him, the other casually dangling.

"During one of the crossings," Petit reminisces, "I lay down on the wire and looked at the sky, and I saw a bird above me."

The tightrope dancer and the bird contemplated each other for a long moment.

"I could see that bird pretty high," Petit says, "and I saw the eyes were red, and I thought of the myth of Prometheus."

Prometheus, I vaguely remember, stole fire from the gods—for which Zeus punished him. But I can't help also thinking of Icarus, who flew on wings of wax too near to the sun.

"The bird," Petit continues, "was looking at me as if I was invading his territory, trespassing—which I was. So at some point I thought the god of the wind, the god of the towers, the god of the wire—all those forces that we persist in thinking don't exist but actually rule our lives—might become impatient, might become annoyed by my persistent vagabondage."

Then I understood. For his transgression, Prometheus was bound to a rock where an eagle fed on his liver, but he did not die. Nor did Petit, thoughtfully considering the limits of his ambition—whereas Icarus, his wings dissolving, fell into the sea and perished.

Petit obeyed his intuition and walked back to the South Tower from which he had begun his extraordinary journey. Reluctantly, he came down from the sky.

Watching this episode—recorded by photographers from the ground as well as the air—I remember how I reacted at the time. With terror and delight. What Petit had done was a kind of aerial poetry.

The night of September 10, 2001, I could barely sleep—waking, turning, dozing, and waking again in a restless cycle of anxiety. I woke up once thinking that if I had an excuse for not meeting my class the next morning, I'd take it. My mind had felt jumbled all day, and I couldn't focus on anything. "But it's just a class," I kept saying to myself. "You'll feel better when it's over."

At last, toward morning—as I often do at that hour—I fell into a dream.

I was in a house that seemed very flimsy—cottage-like and made of wood. It reminded me of a farmhouse in Wisconsin I'd rented with friends for the summer in the late 1970s. Everything was run-down about that house. The roof was fragile, its siding was weathered and gray, and it had no indoor plumbing or heat. The floors sloped, the windows were not square, and the porch was sinking into the ground.

Yet, it was set in a beautiful landscape. Fields of corn or alfalfa (depending on the year) spread like an apron around it, and a small, rippling river ran nearby, close enough for mists to rise from its margins in early summer evenings. A massive barn about a hundred yards away harbored nests of swallows that flew in circles above our heads until it fell to its knees one year—the casualty of a severe thunderstorm. My friends and I made a garden not far from the house, where we raised bumper crops of lettuce, tomatoes, and zucchini. Our little community did not last long, but I remember being happy there.

In my dream, I am not able to make the house secure.

I keep trying to lock the doors, but I can't. The house feels vulnerable to me in a way that makes me anxious. Yet, I do not think of the house as threatening. Rather, I feel as permeable as it. As wildly and helplessly open.

Mother of the Bride

The past only comes back when the present runs so
smoothly that it is like the sliding surface of a deep river.
Then one sees through the surface to the depths. In those
moments I find one of my greatest satisfactions, not that I
am thinking of the past; but that it is then that I am living
most fully in the present.
—Virginia Woolf, *Moments of Being*

When I was in my thirties, I liked to wear my mother's old evening gowns, elegant designer dresses she had worn when she and my father would go out on the town. Or so I imagined. I had no idea where they actually went, but my dad's sleek tux and my mother's filmy gowns conjured images of Fred Astaire and Ginger Rogers hoofing it on Broadway or flying down to Rio. As a child, I pictured my parents like that—a romantic couple toasting each other with champagne in a fancy nightclub or dancing to big band music under the stars.

There's one dress I especially loved. It has a softly draped bodice with a low-cut back and is made of a silvery, satiny material that clings to waist and hips, falling gracefully to the floor. Tropical flowers and greenery shimmer in the folds of the bosom, splashing down the skirt. I wore this dress in the 1970s, when vintage clothing was in style. In it, I felt as sophisticated and beautiful as my once-young mother.

Over time, I found fewer and fewer occasions to wear this dress—until there came a day when I had to admit I'd put on one too many pounds. But I still wasn't able to part with it, moving it from one closet to another in its billowy dry cleaning bag.

At last I had an inspiration. Perhaps Jess might like it?

The dress was still in mint condition. If it had stood out in the 1970s, it was even more remarkable now that glamour was back in vogue—along with martinis and manhattans, the cocktails of my parents' generation.

"What do you think?" I ask Jess, holding the dress up for her inspection. "Would you ever wear it?"

Jess has had a love affair with New York from the time she was eight years old and had a birthday celebration at her father's photography exhibit at the Museum of Modern Art. After graduating from Sarah Lawrence College—which she chose, in part, for its proximity to the city—she moved into a studio apartment on East Houston Street. Now she and Jim live in Brooklyn, and in nine months they will be married.

This is her first visit in several years to Minneapolis, the city where she grew up.

Jess and I are both tall, but she has inherited more of my mother's figure, full in the bosom and slender in the hips.

"It's beautiful," she says, looking at me hesitantly. "Are you sure you don't want it yourself?"

I've been trying to imagine her future with Jim. They like to go out and seem to think nothing of flying to London for a friend's wedding—or to Istanbul for Christmas holiday. The dress will clearly have more of a life with her than me.

"This dress needs to be worn," I say. "You take it."

Later in the spring, when I come to New York for a bridal shower her friend, Christie, and cousin, Robin, have arranged, we talk about her wedding clothes. Jess has already picked out her bridal gown but asks me to go with her to the dressmaker who will alter it.

"I've been looking for something sophisticated," she says, "but not too sexy. It's got a V-neckline that shows some cleavage, but the bosom is covered with a gauze-like material that has ribbons embroidered with tiny flowers, so it looks modest enough. The skirt is fitted and slightly flaring, and there's a cathedral train. It wouldn't be out of place in London but also has the feel of a country wedding."

We are in the subway, balancing our day's purchases on our laps. We've been to several outlet stores where we both tried on various outfits. I couldn't find anything I thought suitable for the mother of the bride, but Jess found a dress for the rehearsal dinner. Like the wedding dress, it needs minor adjustment.

The seamstress is a young, dark-haired Frenchwoman, who owns her own business. Deftly, she extracts Jess's gown from its bag and helps her into it. To me, it looks perfect, but they spend several minutes discussing the height of the neckline (which rubs Jess's collar bone), the extent of the train (too long), and the amount of material in the skirt (not form-fitting enough). Also, what kind of veil will look best? Jess is good at spotting a bargain and has found her dress at a significant markdown. She wonders if she can find a veil on the Internet. The seamstress and I agree that a full-length, custom-made veil will better complement the dress.

In the wedding ceremony, Jim's nine-year-old nephew, Nico, will step on this veil, momentarily stopping the bride in her solemn progress towards the altar. In the video you can see her tilt her head back, a half-smile on her face as she pauses, waiting to be released.

Several months before, Jess and I had visited her grandmother, Nellie May, in Texas, where we all watched a video of an English wedding—for practice, so to speak. The video was provided by Nellie May's caregiver, Trish, a warm-hearted and outspoken British woman who had recently attended the wedding of her niece in the UK. Trish, who is married to a Texan, lives in the town of Electra, a forty-five-minute commute from Nellie May's house. She took care of Nellie May's husband in his last illness and is now providing assistance to Nellie May, whose health is stable, but who needs help moving around.

"It's the hats, you see," Trish says. "All English women wear hats. You've got to find yourself a proper hat."

I've been focusing on the dresses. I have no idea what to wear at a late afternoon wedding. When I was married to Jess's dad, my mother wore a floor-length gown, though the reception was held at our house—in the backyard, where linen-draped tables were set up and a band played music at the end of the driveway next to the garage. We were married at the Old Cathedral in St. Louis, between the famous steel arch and the river, but the reception had a homey feel, with guests filing through the house and out the kitchen door to the yard.

The wedding of Trish's niece took place in a country church, not unlike the one that Jess and Jim have chosen—mainly for its proximity to Brockweir, where the reception will be held in the field below Jim's mother's house. There will be a marquee for the sit-down dinner (and in case of rain), but otherwise guests will gather for the first glass of champagne in the grassy meadow next to the smooth-flowing Wye River.

If English churches look picturesque, it's in part because they are so old. St. Mary the Virgin, where Jess and Jim plan to be married, is a Norman structure, dating from the eleventh century. Made of local stone, it seems wedded to the landscape. Pitted and moss-covered grave markers stand like sentinels guarding its entrance—silent witnesses to the centuries of baptisms, marriages, and deaths that are inscribed in the church's registry. Watching the video of Trish's niece's wedding, I am as fascinated by the setting as I am by the women's soft summer dresses and voile hats, adorned with feathers and flowers and molded into bright shapes.

Out of the blue, I receive a phone message from my graduate school roommate, who was one of the bridesmaids in my first wedding. Her father, an abstract expressionist painter, has been given a posthumous exhibit at a Chelsea Art Gallery in New York City. Would I like to come?

It has been at least ten years since I've heard from Helen, who moved to England after graduate school, settling into a job at the University of East Anglia, where she married, bore two children, divorced, and married again before moving back to the States. Between us, since we first met, we have accumulated four marriages and almost eighty years of life history.

As it happens, the opening coincides with my visit to New York for the wedding shower. Jess is tied up for the evening, so I take a cab into the city, arriving at a blank-faced building whose door blends into the façade. Riding a freight elevator to the third floor, I follow the sound of voices down a narrow hallway into a brightly lit room. My eyes sweep past large canvasses filled with bold strokes and glaring colors—red, green, yellow, black—searching for Helen. At last I spy her, as slim as ever, in a form-fitting plum-colored sheath.

Helen, the quintessential New Yorker, has a distinctive sense of style—and is always impeccably dressed. She has inherited her mother's fashion buyer's eye, along with her father's verve and dash. Standing next to her, I remember how I used to feel when we shared an apartment in New Haven—like the country cousin from the Midwest.

I say hello, brush her cheek with my lips, shake hands with her other guests, then wait for them to move away so we can have a real conversation.

"So Jess is getting married," Helen says at last. "My daughter, Liberty, just got married in England, but I moved back. My husband, Graham—I don't think you've ever met—is convinced that the art market is better here, and I lucked into a good retirement package."

"You missed my second husband completely," I say with a laugh, remembering that Helen's first husband was an architect and the next a painter, like her father.

"Right," says Helen, with a falling tone in her voice that I recognize from the old days, along with the whisper of a British accent. "They go by fast—the years I mean, of course." She leans toward me, touching my arm.

"And how is Frank?"

"We've made peace in our old age."

"Good. My ex and I have nothing in common but our children."

I'd forgotten how direct Helen can be.

"Frank and I . . ." I begin, realizing I don't know how to describe my relationship with Jessica's father. "Frank, well . . . he's . . . well we both adore Jess. She's the best thing I've ever done . . . the best thing that's happened in my life."

"Ah," says Helen, as if this makes perfect sense. "Do you remember when I came to Vermont after she was born? Even as a baby she seemed to take the center of the house."

Helen's words call up vivid images.

The farmhouse we inhabited at the bottom of a steep dirt road, the fields that surrounded it on all sides, and the distant, low-lying mountains. A quiet landscape of extraordinary beauty. I had felt oblivious to it in the midst of my busy life at the time, but this is now what I most clearly remember. The foreground of my life—my daily frustrations and anxieties—have fallen away, while this silent background, revolving slowly through the seasons, remains.

"Yes, I remember that," I say. "It was early spring, when there was still snow on the ground—the kind that's thin and crusty on the surface and melting underneath. You wrote some poems for Jess, and in one of them you gave her a name: 'water under snow.'"

On impulse, I invite Helen to Jessica's wedding shower. I want someone from my past—someone who stood next to me at my own wedding ceremony and who knew my daughter as a baby—to act as a witness to our collective history.

Helen, then and now—despite all the changes we have endured in the years between—seems to represent two compass points in time between which I imagine myself drawing a smooth and continuous arc.

Toward the end of that week, Jess and Jim invite some friends to their apartment for a buffet dinner. As we are getting ready, I urge Jess to try on my mother's dress.

"You said it fits," I remind her. "I'd like to see how it looks. Maybe you can wear it after the wedding—later in the evening, I mean."

"I've thought about that," she says. "But I'm worried I'll spill something on it. Also, it snaps up the side. What if they pull apart while I'm dancing?"

"Let me see it anyway," I say. "You might want to wear it sometime."

While Jess is in the bedroom, her friend, Christie, and cousin, Robin, arrive. Jim asks what they'd like to drink while I explain what Jess is doing.

Then she appears.

With her fair skin and wavy auburn hair, Jess does not resemble my black-haired, olive-skinned mother in any obvious way, but she has her figure. The dress clings to her body as if it had been made for her. As if the dress had skipped a generation and found its rightful owner. As if it has come home.

"It's gorgeous! It's perfect!" Christie and Robin exclaim.

"You have to wear it," I say.

"Well I don't want to damage it. And look at these snaps." Jess swings her body to the side to reveal the delicate articulations of fasteners.

"So what if the dress gets a little mussed?" I say. "What better occasion? And you already have a dressmaker. I'm sure she can replace the snaps with a zipper."

"I agree," says Christie. "It's a fabulous dress, and it fits you like a glove."

"You look terrific," nods Robin.

"Very sexy," adds Jim, joining us from the kitchen with Christie's and Robin's glasses of wine.

"I'll think about it," says Jess.

In the meantime, I worry over my own outfit. I want to wear something nice—without upstaging the bride—to fit in at an English wedding. Yet, I hate to shop, never wear a hat, and am busy all spring teaching my classes. As a result, I put everything off to the last minute.

I find the hat first. It's black straw with a low crown and a wide brim—which will go with anything—and it fits. I have a small head, which looks even smaller in most hats. This one isn't even expensive. In the worst-case scenario, I can just buy another one.

Then I trudge through one store after another, pulling dresses off the rack—too bright, too subdued, too sexy, too sedate. Eventually, I settle on a filmy black silk skirt, which I combine with an off-white sleeveless top and a pale cream organza jacket—all made by a Chinese woman in a specialty shop—and pricey enough that my credit card company calls to be sure I actually want to make this purchase.

The black hat, with a soft-petalled flower pinned to its brim, will do just fine, I think. In London, a few days before the wedding, I find a pair of pointy-toed shoes, with small heels and crisscrossed straps, to complete the effect. At last, I feel satisfied that I'll look OK without calling attention to myself.

Only later do I realize how much I have internalized my daughter's vision of her bridal party.

"In England," she explains, "bridesmaids don't always dress alike. So I picked a raw Indian silk for their skirts—which they can choose in any color—and then they can each pick a white top in any design they want."

In a photograph taken in her hotel dressing room the day of the wedding, we stand on either side of her—her bridesmaids in their blue, orange, and magenta skirts and sheer white blouses and me in my black skirt and pale organdy jacket.

I arrive in London to blustery, rainy weather—not untypical for England at the end of May. The forecast for the weekend—also the weekend of the Queen's Jubilee—is favorable in terms of sun, but who can say?

After a day of shopping, I take a train to Chepstow—the closest stop to Brockweir—where I expect to be met by Jess and Jim, who have already arrived. After an hour or so of waiting and searching the streets, I spy a taxi and approach the driver. I have to get to Brockweir—or Tintern where I am staying—somehow. The driver has been sent by Jess, who is delayed on the freeway, returning from a trip to Bath. But surely she'll be at my lodging in Tintern by the time I arrive.

Not only is Jess nowhere in sight, but there is also no sign of the proprietor—and, to make matters worse, I don't have the right change for my driver. I unload my baggage at the front door and walk down the driveway to a shop below. I'm exchanging bills when Jess, Jim, and Christie drive up. I pay my fare, load my bags into their car, and squeeze in beside them. No place to go but Jim's mother's house in Brockweir.

Shortly after we arrive, Jess's dad drives up with his wife, Lucy, and their two girls, Emma and Grace. They've rented a car and driven straight from Heathrow. By then, the sky has partly cleared, and it's near sunset. We linger outdoors, greeting one another, discussing our respective flights and stretching our legs—Di's five black labs darting excitedly among us.

"Did you find a hat?" Lucy asks. Her emphasis makes it clear that we've gotten the same message about the importance of female headgear.

"Yes, but at the last minute. How about you?"

"Let me show you," she says, walking toward the car and retrieving a light blue straw that is—in all but color—an exact replica of the one I've bought for myself.

I turn the hat over and examine the label to be sure. "I can't believe it," I say. "Mine's the same make, but I got it on the West Coast."

Lucy is different from me in the most obvious ways. She's blonde, petite, and twelve years younger than I; yet, we share the same birthday.

Long ago, I wondered about this coincidence but haven't thought about it in recent years. There are lots of synchronicities in life—many of which are not meaningful—along with ones that speak to hidden wishes and desires. The affair of the hat has no special resonance, as far as I can see. Yet, it is startling.

Perhaps Lucy and I are connected in ways I've never considered? Her girls, Emma and Grace, now in their preteens, are new to my eyes. I haven't seen them since they were babies. I look at them as young-women-to-be, my daughter's half-sisters and members of her wedding party. And somehow connected to me. My ex-stepdaughters? Is there even a word for how we are related?

The light begins to dim, and the air grows chill, so we go inside—where we phone Frank's and my lodgings, with no response. Over wine and hors d'oeuvres with Di, we decide to drive to Nightingale Cottage, where Frank and his family are staying, hoping someone can be roused. We make this trip on two-lane roads bordered by impenetrable hedges, winding upward in fading sunlight until we reach the owner's house at the crest of a hill—where everything is so intensely green that I feel I might run into a Maypole or Morris dancers at any moment. But no one's there.

So we pile back into our cars, looking for a pub Jim has heard about for dinner. After many false turns down roads that narrow and disappear into wildness, we detect a sign flashing dimly in the mist. We enter a timeless, Brigadoon-like space, where we are welcome, warm, and safe. We are the vanguard of the wedding party: Jess, Jim, Christie, Frank, Lucy, Emma, Grace, and me.

In the course of the evening, over sausages and ale, Frank apologizes to me for forgetting my birthday. This is the year we have both turned sixty. I say it's OK.

The next day is full of clouds and partial sun. Di hosts a champagne brunch at her house for the small party that has begun to assemble. I walk from my lodging in Tintern, which is on the west bank of the Wye in Wales, to Brockweir, on the opposite bank in England, crossing a narrow bridge and passing through town until I turn down the dirt lane that leads to Di's house. There, I greet Jim's sister, Lucy, and her nine-year-old son, Nico, who have just arrived from Florida.

We are an eclectic bunch, yet we are beginning to form the nucleus of a new family constellation—one that includes too many divorces, separations, and remarriages to enumerate—but which starts to make a kind of sense.

We assemble in the oldest part of Di's house, the part dating back to the eighth century, where we fill our plates with cheese, fruit, and crackers and raise our glasses of champagne. The field below the house where the marquee will be erected in two days is sodden, and everyone is concerned about this. Weather forecasts for the weekend are holding up, but nothing is certain.

"We've arranged for a bank of taxis," Jess says, "to take guests home. And we have tractors ready also to tow cars that get stuck in the field."

"Have you heard about the vicar?" Di's clear, trilling voice breaks through our conversation. She is talking with the two Lucys (her daughter and Frank's wife) about her trip to the church to discuss the flower arrangements.

"He's run away with another woman," I quip, before pausing to think.

"Really," Di says straight-faced, "there's been a scandal. We went expecting to talk with him, but he's left the parish. He's been having an affair, and it's gotten out, so he had to leave rather abruptly. He left word he'd be back for the wedding, though."

All of a sudden, I feel as if I'm in a wickedly funny British sit-com. What next?

Just then, we all hear a sharp report, quickly followed by a child's scream. Oh no, I say to myself—scanning the room with a mother's eye for who is missing.

Emma, her red hair flying and pale skin flushing, dashes into the room, throwing herself into her mother's arms—where she bursts into tears.

"I didn't mean to," she says. "We didn't know. Really, I'm so sorry."

"What is it?" Lucy says calmly. "Tell us what happened."

"The gun went off," she says breathlessly, "but we didn't think it was loaded—I swear."

By now, Di has left the room, moving instinctively in the direction of the sound. A moment later, she returns to the room with Nico, who fixes his gaze on the floor.

"It was my air-rifle," Di says. "There was a blank in it. Thank goodness no one was hurt. But that was very naughty of you, Nico. You know better than that. You must never touch Granny's gun."

"He didn't mean to," says Emma, defending him. "I asked him to show it to me, and I thought it was safe to pull the trigger." Emma starts to cry again at the thought of what might have happened.

Seeing Emma's tears, Nico begins to cry also.

Everyone can see that the children are as distressed as we are relieved.

"All right," says Jim, stepping in. "Let's have a talk, Nico," drawing him away from the startled adults into another room, while Lucy continues to hold Emma, murmuring into her hair, alternately soothing and chastising her.

Later, as the sky continues to clear, we move outside to the terrace, where we scan the horizon and the swiftly moving brown river in the distance, then bend to inspect the brightly blooming flowers. Jim sets up a croquet game for the children on the adjacent lawn and plays with them for a while. It is sunny, no one has been harmed, and we have found a lull in time, like a small eddy in the river, where we can all relax. For a moment, there is nothing much to say or do. So we watch the children, sip champagne, comment on the budding flowers, and pose for one another's snapshots.

The next morning, Frank, Lucy, and the girls are planning a drive to Bristol—to the tailor shop where Frank will be fitted for the morning suit he has rented. In the meantime, Frank's niece, Jamie, and her brother, Lloyd, arrive from Germany.

Their parents can't leave their ranch in Oklahoma, but Jamie and Lloyd have been traveling in Europe together and have just left a horse show, where Jamie has been demonstrating her skills as a trainer and rider.

Jamie, who has a wide-open, Texas kind of face and is down-to-earth and practical like her mother, quickly establishes herself as everyone's designated driver. By the time she arrives from London, she has not only mastered the skill of driving on the opposite side of the road but also seems to have an internal Global Positioning System that keeps her oriented. I recognize competence when I see it and attach myself to her instinctively.

Lloyd, two years younger than Jamie, is more of a wild card. He's a guy's guy, into the culture of sports and bars and college sophomore life. He's something of a soccer star but hasn't really figured out what he wants to do with himself. Jamie, in contrast, has always known what she wants: to ride, board, and train horses like her mom and dad. Together, they sound a quintessentially American note in this old world, English setting. And I love them for it.

"Do you mind if I come with you to Bristol?" I ask. "There's something I'd like to read at the rehearsal dinner—just a quote from Shakespeare or Virginia Woolf—but I didn't think to bring any books with me."

It's not traditional for mothers to offer toasts at an English wedding, but Jim, sensing that I want to be included, has suggested that I might want to say something the night before. I leap at this opportunity but feel anxious without a text.

Also, something about the gathering of the wedding party has jogged a memory of Woolf's *To the Lighthouse*. There's a passage that has been nagging at me for a couple of days, in which an ordinary dinner party suddenly becomes a perfectly formed moment. Behind this memory lies a beautiful little scene toward the end of *The Tempest*, in which Prospero, knowing he is about to lose his daughter to the dashing young Ferdinand, stages a pageant with the goddesses Iris, Juno, and Ceres to bless the bridal couple.

Without one of these great authors to back me up, I'm afraid I'll become tongue-tied.

"There's bound to be a good bookstore in Bristol," I explain.

"Sure," says Frank. "The more the merrier. Come along."

We—the girls and women—spend the morning assembling favors for the wedding dinner. By now, Jess's cousin, Robin, has arrived from Scotland, where she's been traveling with her boyfriend, Shawn. She drives up to Nightingale Cottage, where we're all busily engaged in stuffing sparklers into glassine envelopes with Jess's and Jim's names stamped on them. We fix them to stiff paper backing, along with a sprig of lavender, and then tie it all together with threads of silver ribbon. We've got over a hundred of these to assemble in a couple of hours, so we all bend to the task.

"It's a cottage industry," Lucy observes dryly.

Finally, we are done. The favors lie neatly stacked in a box, and we are free for the afternoon. We pile into two cars— Frank, Lucy, and the girls in one and Jamie, Lloyd, and me in the other (Robin opts for a nap at her hotel)—for the hour's drive to Bristol.

The first stop is the tailor shop, Moss Brothers, where Frank will get his final fitting. We crowd into the tiny store, some- what to the dismay of the proprietors, who are used to a quieter clientele. Lloyd shops for a jacket while Frank disap- pears into a back room. I've already spied a bookstore just up the street.

Gradually we disperse. Jamie needs to find an accessory for her wedding outfit and plans to explore Bristol on her own. Lucy is interested in strolling down the street. We agree to meet two hours later.

Unexpectedly, I find Emma and Grace following me.

"What are those books you're looking for?" Emma asks, as we enter Blackwells. "I can help, if you want."

"One is a play by Shakespeare," I explain. "It's called *The Tempest*. The other is a novel by a woman named Virginia Woolf."

"OK," she says. "I'll go look for Shakespeare." She disappears into the back of the store with Grace in tow.

It doesn't take me long to find a paperback edition of *To the Lighthouse*—a text that I own in hardcover and don't want to pay too much for in duplicate. I locate the cheapest edition and page through to the passage I remember. I'm reading it when Emma appears beside me.

"Look," she says. "I found these. Which one do you want?"

Emma has located two different editions of *The Tempest*, both of which she hands to me carefully.

"Thanks," I say, looking at her closely. I'm surprised—and also gratified—that she has taken me so seriously. She's a beautiful girl, I observe with a pang. I'd always wanted more than one child. Lucy is fortunate, I think.

"I really appreciate this," I tell her. "I'll look at both and then decide."

"OK," says Emma, in an off-hand way. "I'll wait for Dad up front with Grace."

What I know about Frank—from being married to him—is that he is chronically late, so I don't rush to pay for my purchase. Instead, I wander through various sections of the store, which has several levels, until I begin to grow impatient. Not only have I not seen Emma or Grace for nearly an hour, but there's no sign of Frank. I decide to go to the front desk to wait.

"Oh, there you are," I hear at last. "We've been looking for you."

It seems that Frank has been in the store for quite some time. He's found Emma and Grace but hasn't seen me. We've been searching for—and missing—each other for about half an hour.

"Great," I say. "Let's go. How about Jamie, Lloyd, and Lucy?" It's getting late, and we need to get back.

"Lucy went to a bookstore down the street," Frank says, "and Lloyd said he'd meet us about now."

As we exit the store, Jamie and Lloyd approach from different directions. Now we're only missing Lucy. Suddenly Frank spies her across the street. She's standing in front of the Moss Brothers store, shouting and waving her arms. But the traffic has grown too thick for us to hear.

"Your camera," I detect, above the roar, as she raises the object in question.

Frank starts across the street to reach her. I'm about two paces behind. All at once, I spy a furiously peddling bicyclist turn the corner and head our way. Lucy is still waving—but now more frantically. Frank is determined to reach her. He and the mad cyclist are on a collision course.

"Frank!" I shout. "Stop!"

Because I am right behind him, Frank hears me. He pauses, turns his head, and the cyclist rushes past.

We continue our crossing and reach the other side—where Lucy explains that Frank had left his camera in the tailor shop and that someone had seen her on the street and recognized her. She was trying to catch his attention when the cyclist appeared out of nowhere.

What does it take to survive a wedding?

More guests arrive. Jess's friend, Melissa (one of her bridesmaids), and her husband, Prester, show up at The Moon and Sixpence, a pub in Tintern, where a group is beginning to gather for dinner.

Jess, Christie, Robin, and Melissa cluster at one table while Lucy, Jamie, and I sit at another. Lloyd roams the room with a DV camera, sweeping the scene and occasionally zeroing in for closer scrutiny. Frank is in his element, greeting each newcomer with a glass of ale in hand and waving them into the room. Emma and Grace flit from one table to another, too excited to settle anywhere.

The Moon and Sixpence is a small tavern; just a couple of rooms with low-beamed ceilings, a dark-paneled bar, and a small kitchen behind. A chalkboard over the bar announces the main menu. We're stretching their capacity, but no one complains. A single waitress circulates among us, refilling glasses of wine or ale, patiently taking and serving orders.

Jim's dad, Simon, and his wife, Lynne, who have just flown in from Toronto, enter along with Jim's sister, Lucy. Di, who is worrying over every last-minute detail of the flowers and the field, has decided to turn in early. The workers are due to arrive at an ungodly hour in the morning to set up the marquee. Jim stays home, knowing he will also need to be up betimes.

Simon heads for the bar to order a round of drinks, while Lynne slips into an empty chair at my table. Lynne is British, but she has lived most of her life in Canada. Her accent is soft, and she seems somehow "American" to me.

"Tell me what's been happening," she says, looking from me to Lucy with lively interest.

Lucy begins describing the trip to Bristol when I hear another story breaking through.

At the table next to us, Jess and Christie are recounting their experience of 9/11. I try to focus on what Lucy is saying while straining to eavesdrop on the conversation next to me.

It's Christie's voice that I hear.

"We were meeting," she says, "and I was a little late . . . and I looked out of my apartment window, and I saw all these people running down Broadway . . ."

I glance over at their table. Jess is looking down, her face expressionless. Melissa, sitting next to her, so close that their shoulders touch, lifts a hand, then lets it drop.

"I knew there was something terribly wrong—and I was frantic . . . I kept phoning Jess . . ."

I begin to understand how Christie must have felt—living so close to Ground Zero, not knowing what was happening to her—or her friend.

"I've had this sense of foreboding," Robin says suddenly, "for so long. It's as if my life has been too easy, as if something terrible will happen to make up, to compensate."

How has 9/11, like an unwelcome guest, broken into this moment of celebration? I sit quietly, listening to Lucy's story of our trip to Bristol, while also attending to the conversation at the next table. The two strands of narrative blend with each other in my mind. Like two sides of a mirror, flipping back and forth, one image the obverse of the other.

After eating and drinking for a while, we all shift tables. I'm feeling tired. It's just a short walk from the pub to my B&B up the road, so I can leave anytime, but I don't want to appear inhospitable.

I find myself sitting with Lynne and Jim's sister, Lucy.

Lucy, like Jim, is tall, fair-haired, and athletically slim. She's a midwife and massage therapist who's committed to an organic, holistic lifestyle. I'm impressed by her and also a little intimidated.

I gush about the landscape and how much I love Wordsworth—Tintern Abbey being so close. I am feeling more and more foolish.

"Oh," she says, "I could lend you my school text. I'm sure it's in my room somewhere."

"That's OK," I say. "Really, I don't want to bother you."

Gradually we find a common language. Lucy lives in Florida, so she knows something about the American idiom.

By the end of the evening, Lucy has invited me to join her on a walk to Devil's Pulpit—where I will have an excellent view of Tintern Abbey.

I don't tell her I've already done this walk. Instead, I accept with pleasure, happy to be taken under her wing.

The next morning is clearer than the day before, but high clouds move swiftly overhead threatening the possibility of rain. Once again, I walk from my B&B in Tintern to Di's place in Brockweir, the route now familiar. I have to be careful crossing the roadway in front of my lodging, as there are curves that hide oncoming traffic from both directions, but otherwise I'm confident of my way.

The house is in a bustle when I arrive. The field has been freshly mowed, the marquee is now up, and Di is busy supervising the flower arrangements for the church. She waves us out of the house for our walk to Devil's Pulpit, no doubt happy to have a moment to herself.

Jess, Jim, Lucy, and I gather raingear from the mudroom, then head toward Offa's Dyke Path, the strenuous uphill trek I'm now familiar with. But this time it's another season, with everything newly green and budding. The sky darkens, and drops of rain plunk onto my slicker as I set myself a steady pace I feel I can maintain. Jess, Jim, and Lucy are already well ahead of me.

Suddenly, I notice a black lab at my side—then another, and another, until all five of Di's dogs cluster around me, dancing forward, then turning around to follow me for a few steps before moving ahead once again. They continue this complex choreography until Jess, Jim, and Lucy notice.

"Look," says Jess, "they're following Mom as if she's Di."

"She's wearing Mum's jacket," Jim observes.

"Probably catches her scent," says Lucy.

"I just grabbed a coat off the hook," I say, realizing that I've become a Di surrogate. In my long-sleeved slicker, with the hood pulled up, I must look—and smell—like the dog's master and caretaker.

They circle around me, running ahead, returning, prancing at my side, until we reach the summit. Today, I'm the Artemis of the walk, the local goddess of this wood.

As we arrive at the clearing from which we can view Tintern Abbey—in long shot as it were—Lucy tells me that the outcropping of rock that defines this space is thought to be a Druid site. Sacrifices may have once been offered here.

Lucy believes in things I cannot see—and which I'm not sure I assent to—but at this particular moment, in this time and place, what she says makes sense to me. A power that is not human seems to permeate this landscape. I can understand why Druids may have worshipped features of geography, like rocks or trees, instead of an image made in their likeness.

The sun begins to break through, illuminating the valley below—not only Tintern Abbey in the distance, but also the dazzling white expanse of tent in Di's field. Billowing in the wind, the marquee reflects the light flashing from the sky.

My heart bumps, catches, and lurches forward.

My daughter is going to be married.

The Wedding Party

Now all the candles were lit up, and the faces on both sides
of the table were brought nearer by the candle light, and
composed, as they had not been in the twilight, into a party
round a table, for the night was now shut off by panes
of glass, which, far from giving any accurate view of the
outside world, rippled it so strangely that here, inside the
room, seemed to be order and dry land; there, outside, a
reflection in which things waved and vanished, waterily.
—Virginia Woolf, *To the Lighthouse*

Two nights before my daughter's wedding, I find myself
talking with her dad at the cottage where he, Lucy,
and the girls are staying. We've had very little communication since our divorce, especially since he moved from
Minnesota to Massachusetts the same year that Jess went
away to college. Yet, I still feel a part of his family, mainly due to his mother, Nellie May, who has drawn me back
into the fold. As a result, I'm comfortable with Jess's aunts
and uncles and her first cousins. But I still feel somewhat
awkward around Frank. We were never very good at conversation, knowing so little about life in our twenties and
early thirties—when we met, married, and divorced—that
we didn't know what to say. We haven't done much better
since.

The cottage, situated at the crest of a hill with views in all directions, is so tiny that it makes me think of something out of a fairy tale. Like the house of the three bears or the seven dwarves. Jess and Jim are home with Di tonight, working on a seating chart for the wedding dinner, but many other guests are here: Robin and her boyfriend, Shawn; Jamie and Lloyd; Melissa and Prester; and Sally Dixon, an artist from Minneapolis who has known Jess from the time she was three years old.

Sally, who is a few years older than Frank and me, is one of those women whose beauty is timeless. She has high cheekbones, intensely blue eyes, and hair that gleams like spun silver. Her personality is even more compelling. A sophisticated woman with a complex history, Sally expresses her feelings warmly and radiates kindness.

Even though I haven't seen much of her over the years—she was more Frank's friend than mine—I'm glad she's here. Like my graduate school friend Helen, she forms a link with my past, in this case, my years as a young mother in Minneapolis.

Frank, Sally, and I are talking in the kitchen, where Frank is chopping tomatoes for spaghetti sauce. I'm on my second glass of wine and beginning to relax.

"Jess is such a beautiful young woman," Sally comments, swirling the ruby wine in her goblet before taking a sip. "I can't believe how much she has grown up. I remember her as a teenager—and of course she was beautiful then too—coming to art openings in Minneapolis. But now she's absolutely stunning."

"She wasn't so happy then," I say, remembering those years from a different perspective. "She was angry with both of us—for good reason, I guess. We didn't exactly have our act together."

Frank and I both remarried in the middle of her high school years. Preoccupied with our own wishes and designs, we hardly noticed the impact of our choices on Jess. She was furious.

Frank, who is busily stirring the sauce, looks doubtful. Maybe I should speak for myself?

"But look at her now," Sally says, her blue eyes shining. "Something has obviously come out right."

Later that evening, we arrange ourselves in a rough circle in the small, low-ceilinged living room with our paper plates balanced on our laps. Frank, who has been busy serving everyone, takes the only empty seat, next to me. For a few minutes, we make small talk about the wedding.

When we've covered this ground, I ask about his recently diagnosed sleep apnea—something I've heard about from Jess.

"I went to this sleep clinic," he says, "where they monitored me all night. Lucy was complaining about my snoring. Do you remember that?"

"No," I say, "I don't," wondering if I've deliberately suppressed such a memory—or if the snoring problem is recent. "But I do remember how you used to fall asleep at the oddest moments—like at plays or concerts."

"Or when I was driving late . . ."

"Like your dad."

"Well now there's an explanation. They've given me a mask to wear at night that keeps me breathing evenly."

"I'm glad," I say, mischievously adding, "I used to think that when you fell asleep in the evening you were bored with me."

Frank gives me a rueful smile, then changes the subject.

"I'm sorry about your mother's death."

Though we talked on the phone when this happened, I'm a little taken aback.

"She died the way she wanted to," I say, "at home and without any invasive procedures. I knew it was going to happen—and I think she did too—though we couldn't talk about any of this. I never found a way to get close to her. But I miss her."

"I know," says Frank.

"What about your father? Were you there when he died? I wish I could have been with my mother, but it didn't work out that way."

"I was there not long before. Lucy and I flew down with Emma, who was just a baby. We went in to him, and I held Emma up so he could see her. He wasn't able to talk by then. But he put his hand out and touched her leg and held it there for a while. So he knew he had another grandchild."

"That's good," I say.

Frank's younger daughter, Grace, who is more guarded than her sister, Emma, and who has been observing us from across the room, comes over to find out what we're talking about. She sits cross-legged on the floor in front of us, listening. Once she realizes we're talking about death, she gets up and goes back to her mother, who's engaged in a lively conversation with Sally. Grace is too young to think about ghosts—especially in the midst of a wedding.

The next day is busy with last-minute arrangements. Some kind of outdoor lights are needed to guide guests to the portable loo but also to keep them from wandering too close to the river. Frank and Lloyd are driving to a garden supply store to see what they can find. Since I don't have anything else to do, I offer to go with them.

This wedding is a truly collaborative effort—with all of the parents and stepparents making a financial contribution, in addition to some kind of material labor. Jess and her friend, Christie, have been in charge of the basic arrangements (the church, the marquee, catering, website with travel and housing information for guests, etc.), but the rest of us have all pitched in. Part of my job has involved finding a designer to produce letterpress invitations and mailing them to the American guests. Jim's dad and stepmother, Lynne, have taken charge of the rehearsal dinner, along with champagne and wine for the reception. Di has sent invitations to the British guests, created a design for the wedding program, provided the location for the reception and flowers for the church. In addition, Frank and I have agreed to host a post-wedding brunch at a local pub. Everyone seems equally involved.

Nothing about this wedding—except for the Church of England service—is strictly traditional in its arrangements, yet everything seems to be working. Still, it's hard to feel useful when you're staying at a guesthouse. So I'm glad to accompany Frank and Lloyd on this last-minute errand.

Frank is driving—and mostly he's adapted to the right brain, left-brain kinds of reversal required by English cars and roads. Occasionally, he drifts out of his lane, however, and I'm there to remind him, making a mental note that it's essential, when driving in Britain, to have another person along. I'm glad I did not opt to rent a car on my own.

Lloyd, in the back seat, seems oblivious to the kind of road hazards I so vividly imagine. He's a college kid, I remind myself, who's still into drinking, danger, and fast cars.

None of us seems very clear about where we are going, but I spy a road sign along the way—somewhere on the Welsh side of the river—that reads "Brynmawr," pointing in a direction opposite to the one where we are headed.

The college I attended in the early 1960s is called Bryn Mawr—named for this Welsh town. It seems as if I am going backwards and forwards at the same time—as if my deep past is flashing before my eyes, along with the fleeing landscape.

This double vision—paired with the fact that I'm in the no-man's land of travel—makes me feel as if I'm carrying my entire history with me into the present moment. It also feels something like fate. Why else would I have gone to Bryn Mawr than to wind up here, at a crossroad in Wales, on a quest for garden lights?

We're an improbable crew for this job, given that none of us knows the way to the Garden Center. Yet, it emerges before our eyes—like the pub out of the mist on my first night—in broad daylight, with a huge sign above a warehouse-like building that reminds me of the Home Depot chain of stores in the States. Frank and Lloyd go in search of electric lights to line the path to the loo, while I look for something to warn guests away from the river. We agree on a time to meet near the entrance; otherwise, it will take hours to locate each other in such a vast expanse.

Frank and Lloyd find exactly what they are looking for, while I can only come up with primitive stakes with kerosene-soaked ends. These will produce a steady flame, but they are like medieval torches and somewhat hazardous. Also, the Garden Center is in short supply. We buy all of them—along with the footpath lights—and depart. It's getting close to the time for the church rehearsal, and we must get back.

Frank drops me off at the B&B where I'm staying with Christie, with just enough time to dress before Jess arrives to drive us to the church in St. Briavels. Here we are at last—mothers, fathers, stepmothers, bridesmaids and groomsmen, sister, half-sisters, and nephew—the core wedding party assembled in one place. Even the wayward vicar has arrived on time, no doubt oblivious to our jokes about his behavior.

I take a seat beside Lucy as we watch Frank escort Jess to the altar. In a British wedding, the bridesmaids and ring bearer follow the bride. By now, I am familiar with the order of service, as Jess and I have discussed it many times over the phone—which hymns to sing (three instead of two, to accommodate Jim's wish to include a naval hymn in honor of his deceased grandfather) and three readings: St. Paul's first letter to the Corinthians (endorsed by the vicar, me, and Jess's grandmother), a poem by the sixteenth-century poet Christopher Marlowe that begins "Come live with me and be my love," and "A Birthday," by the nineteenth-century poet Christina Rossetti, each stanza of which ends with the refrain "My love has come to me."

It has taken a lot of time, thought, and negotiation to arrive at this order. One of the things I learned along the way is how hard it is to find poems that honor love in a celebratory way. Most include feelings of bitterness, sadness, or loss.

I'm listening to the first reading when suddenly something seems odd. The language does not feel familiar. I glance at Lucy to see if she's picking up the same clues. She raises her eyebrows as Jess's cousin, Robin, continues to read from the pulpit. All at once, I realize what is wrong. She's not reading from the King James translation of St. Paul's letter to the Corinthians—the one with the beautiful language about how we "now see through a glass darkly, but then face to face," but from some modern version. Silently, Lucy and I disapprove. Frank turns around from his place in the pew in front of us, looking quizzical. This isn't what any of us had expected.

Emboldened by this mute collaboration, I wait until all three readings are done and then approach Jess, who is sitting next to Jim in a pew across the aisle.

"This isn't the text we chose," I say. "What has happened to the King James version?"

Jess, who is in a fine state of nerves by now, hasn't noticed the difference. I realize my mistake. What is important to me is not important to her, and now she's caught in a conflict between me and the vicar.

"I don't know," she says, in a whisper.

By now, the vicar has taken notice of our conversation. He comes over to investigate.

"It's just that we were expecting the King James Version of St. Paul's letter," I say, in my most conciliatory manner.

"Well," he says, "I'm glad you mentioned that. You see the modern text uses the word 'love,' instead of the archaic word 'charity' when referring to the most important of all virtues, and I thought that an American audience, in particular, would not understand this distinction."

My memory of this text goes, "And now abideth faith, hope and charity, these three, but the greatest of these is charity."

"I'm an American," I say, bristling on behalf of my compatriots, "and I know what charity means."

Suddenly I am falling—like an unsuspecting Alice—down a rabbit hole of memory. I'm back in high school at morning chapel service, silently rebelling against the Protestant hymns and prayers, so foreign to my midwestern Catholic upbringing. It's my stepfather who has insisted that I attend this private school for girls, whose principal was educated at Cambridge and who has changed his title to "headmaster." His name is Ronald Beasley, and, as a raw freshman, I have no reason to respect him. He's like my stepfather, an intruder into the life I've known so far. Yet, both of these men will shape my future—in ways I cannot anticipate, much less appreciate, as a resentful fifteen-year-old.

How has my long-ago experience of chapel service in a suburb of St. Louis led me to this moment? How have I become a defender of King James?

I draw a deep breath as Jess glances over her shoulder at me, frowning.

"What I mean is that I don't think Americans will misunderstand. And the traditional language is so beautiful."

"But you see, I've constructed my homily around the idea of love—to resonate, don't you see, with the passage from Corinthians. It's all coordinated. The theme is love; it's all about love."

The comedy of this situation begins to register. Here I am, an American, defending the seventeenth-century King James translation of St. Paul's letter to the Corinthians against an English country vicar. One who has just been disgraced in his own parish and who intends to instruct us all—on the occasion of my daughter's wedding—on the significance of love.

By now, Frank has come over to intervene.

"I agree," he says, in his muted Texas accent. "There won't be a problem with your homily. Most Americans will understand that charity means love."

"Well," the vicar concedes, "I could insert a clarification— for those who might not."

Jess's face loses its worried look. The King James crisis has passed.

Frank, who has not had time to dress for the rehearsal dinner, goes back to his cottage to change, while the rest of us drive to the Parva Inn in Tintern, where the other members of the wedding party have begun to assemble. As if to confirm all our best wishes, the sun, which has been playing hide-and-seek over the course of the afternoon, breaks through for a brilliant and radiant decline.

For the last two days, I've been trying to decide whether to read from Virginia Woolf or Shakespeare this evening, when all of a sudden it occurs to me that the little scene in *The Tempest* is a mini-drama with three distinct parts. Maybe Emma and Grace would like to read it with me tomorrow at the wedding supper? I'm assuming there will be many toasts then, and Shakespeare's little blessing seems especially appropriate to the pastoral setting of the field.

I'm in a state of pre-wedding euphoria, where I'm in love with everyone—like Frankie in Carson McCullers's *The Member of the Wedding*. But in my case, I'm not just in love with the bridal couple but with the entire wedding party—not only Jess and Jim, but also Jim's mother, Di; his father, Simon, and stepmother, Lynne; his sister, Lucy, and nephew, Nico; my ex-husband, Frank; his wife, Lucy; and above all perhaps, their lovely daughters, Emma and Grace.

It's as if I want to hold us all in this exquisite—and fluid—moment of connection as long as possible. We are like dancers, learning our movements as we perform them in careful and silent attunement. Woolf has said this better than me, so I decide to read the passage from *To the Lighthouse* over dinner.

At the same time, I don't want to give up on Shakespeare. On impulse, I approach Lucy with my idea of a joint reading of the blessing from *The Tempest*.

"It sounds interesting," she says pragmatically. "Why don't you ask Frank—and Emma and Grace?"

Emma, who is nearly at my side, has been part-listening, and now she comes close. Grace follows her shyly.

"What is it about?" Emma says.

"Well, it's a blessing spoken by three goddesses."

"Do you have it with you? Can I see it?"

"Yes," I say, drawing the small text out of my purse and handing it to her.

"I see," she says, after a moment's pause. "You can be Iris," pointing to me, "and Grace can be Juno, and I can be Ceres."

I am startled by the swiftness of Emma's decision and by her directorial acumen.

"Can I borrow this?" she says. "Grace and I can study it overnight."

"Of course," I say. "Please take it."

Later in the evening, at the encouragement of Jim, who is seated next to me, I stand to deliver my toast. I say things I remember now only dimly—about how we are creating something together this week by our presence, out of the love we feel for Jess and Jim—about how we are in a complex choreography that is bumpy at moments, like a country dance, but which, like an American Quaker hymn, somehow comes out right. And then I read from Woolf:

> If it were fine, they should go for a picnic. Everything seemed possible. Everything seemed right. Just now (but this cannot last, she thought, dissociating herself from the moment while they were all talking about boots) just now she had reached security; she hovered like a hawk suspended; like a flag floated in an element of joy which filled every nerve of her body fully and sweetly, not noisily, solemnly rather, for it arose, she thought, looking at them all eating there, from husband and children and friends; all of which rising in this profound stillness (she was helping William Bankes to one very small piece more, and peered into the depths of the earthenware pot) seemed now for no special reason to stay there like a smoke, like a fume rising upwards, holding them safe together.

At this point, I begin to lose my nerve. My voice falters, and tears start into my eyes. To steady myself, I place my right hand on Jim's shoulder. All safety—as it did to Woolf—feels fragile to me. With Jim's hard shoulder blade, like the granite outcropping at Devil's Pulpit, under my hand, I continue:

> Nothing need be said; nothing could be said. There it was, all round them. It partook, she felt, carefully helping Mr. Bankes to a specially tender piece, of eternity; as she had already felt about something different once before that afternoon; there was a coherence in things, a stability; something, she meant, is immune from change, and shines out (she glanced at the window with its ripple of reflected lights) in the face of the flowing, the fleeting, the spectral, like a ruby; so that again tonight she had the feeling she had had once today, already, of peace, of rest. Of such moments, she thought, the thing is made that endures.

When I read this passage, I believe it to be true of us—of our little impromptu gathering in the deepening glow of a late spring evening on the border between England and Wales. My whole life, I also believe, has led me to this moment. But then, I'm also a woman in love—with my daughter and her wedding party.

The morning of the wedding passes quickly. Jess and her bridesmaids drive to the next village to have their hair, make-up, and nails done, then gather at a hotel in Tintern to dress. Frank and Lloyd attend to the electric lights and torches in the field. I spend a leisurely morning at my B&B, drinking coffee in the small, terraced garden and writing in my journal. At last, it's time. I shower, dress, arrange my make-up and hair, and step out onto the bend of road that separates me from the wedding hotel. In my fashionable London shoes, I'm walking gingerly, attending to the tarry road.

A car appears out of nowhere, swooping down on me from the left. I look up, startled, and hop to my right. But the car, anticipating a collision, has made a compensating move in the same direction. I stop, momentarily transfixed. The sleek black auto is bearing down on me, but I don't know which way to move—much less how to move quickly in my delicate, pointed shoes. I feel like a squirrel, dashing first one way, then another, baffling the motorist, who is equally confused. At the last minute, he brakes to a stop, allowing me to cross.

One more miss! How would it look if the mother of the bride were run over by a car on her way to the wedding? Feeling foolish, I walk stiffly and carefully on the side of the narrow, two-lane road until I reach the hotel.

When I arrive, everyone is in a flurry. The bridesmaids, already dressed in their bright skirts and sheer, white tops, are assisting Jess into her gown. Someone pops a bottle of champagne, and we all raise our glasses as Jess puts the finishing touches to her make-up. One of the bridesmaids leans over her at the cosmetic mirror to fix the cathedral-length bridal veil into her chignon.

Then her dad arrives with Lucy, Emma, and Grace. He's got a camera with a serious lens hanging around his neck and begins to snap pictures right and left. I've got my little automatic Olympus and am sneaking in as many shots as I can. A photo frenzy ensues. Everybody wants a memento of the occasion. It's a little room for so many people—all of us sipping champagne, fluttering around Jess, hugging, smiling, and saying "cheese." Until it stops.

The time has come. We must all go to the church.

The service is about an hour—long enough for the solemnity of the occasion—yet so fleeting that it is hard for me to recall in retrospect.

Is the bride beautiful?

Is the groom handsome?

Do they say their vows clearly and with feeling?

Yes, yes, and yes.

We say The Lord's Prayer—no matter what we believe. The children's choir sings "All Through the Night," a traditional Welsh song, while the wedding party signs the church register. And suddenly it's over, the steeple bells chiming wildly as we emerge into the blinding late-afternoon sun.

A childhood friend, who was my maid of honor in my long-ago wedding to Frank, drives me, with her husband, to Brockweir for the reception. Elizabeth and I grew up in the same neighborhood in St. Louis and have known each other since high school. She's the director of a major hospital emergency room there. Her second husband, Reid, is a research hematologist.

Though my friend Helen, who was also in my wedding party, was not able to come for the wedding, Elizabeth is here—providing a living, breathing link with my past. Two other friends, who represent that time in my life, have also made the transatlantic journey. My friend, Gail, whom I met as an undergraduate at Bryn Mawr and who was my roommate for two years in graduate school at Yale, has come with her husband, Tom, whom I've known almost as long. And Julian, also a friend from graduate school—who was a groomsman in my first wedding—is here with his third wife, Sophie.

With both parents dead and so little family—neither of my brothers was able to make the trip—I'm thankful for these friends, who give a feeling of continuity to my fractured history. They are like marathon runners, lightly bearing my memories over rough terrain, through radical alterations of space and time, delivering them safely into the present. At the reception in the field, now golden in the late afternoon light, I seek them out—grateful for their fidelity.

But before I walk down to the meadow, I stop to talk with Di, who is standing in the gravel parking area close to the house. I want to thank her for her hospitality and to express some of my pent-up feelings about the wedding ceremony. She's in close conversation with her daughter, Lucy.

"How rude," Lucy says.

"What happened?" I inquire.

"Someone arrived in a taxi from London, just as we were leaving for the church, with no money to pay the driver," Lucy says, looking at me and raising her eyebrows.

"Oh, no," I say.

"And then she wanted to take a shower in the house," adds Di.

"Mum called Jim, who told her to say no, but of course she couldn't," explains Lucy, glancing sideways at her mother.

I can well imagine Di's dilemma. She was exasperated and about to leave for the church, yet her perfect manners made it impossible for her to refuse a guest.

"Guess what happened next?" Lucy says.

"The dogs," Di interpolates, "got into the sitting room and savaged the cake." Her expression is equivocal—as if she is either about to cry or burst into laughter.

Though I haven't yet seen this cake, I've heard about it: how elegant it is, how much Jess paid for it, and how it was transported with care all the way from Bristol to be stored in Di's sitting room until the time of the reception. At Jess's urging, I shopped in London for a lace tablecloth to display it.

"I can't believe this," I say, torn between outrage and amusement. I can't help thinking of Di's exuberant black labs wanting to take part in the wedding party in the only way they can.

"We're going to pin a napkin over the damaged part," says Lucy practically. "It's really not that visible if you turn the good side to the front."

When I get to the marquee, I go straight to the cake, which stands regally on its round, linen-clad table next to the entrance. It is a marvel of culinary art, with vines and flowers twining up each of its several tiers, culminating in a series of delicate, open-throated lilies. I can understand how Jess blew her budget for such a beautiful object. A damask napkin masks the rear. Lifting it, I see what the dogs have done. Several gouges reveal the cake's rich, chocolaty interior. Its smooth and perfect façade is broken by an expression of raw appetite. Perhaps the dogs are telling us something by their attack on the cake. This, too, may be what we are celebrating. It does not matter, in any case. The dogs, though now safely confined to the house, have made their mark.

Much later in the evening, one of them (sick with sugar, no doubt) vomits on the shoes of one of my friends, who accepts Di's invitation to view the house. This, too, seems appropriate. Weddings are full of wild and unpredictable energy. Though framed by ritual, they are inherently messy and imperfect.

While the cake's seamless beauty has been marred, the weather could not be more dreamily perfect. Despite weeks of rain— with high blowing clouds and scattered, though lessening, showers leading up to the evening of the rehearsal dinner— the wedding day itself dawns bright and clear. And stays that way—suspended in a moment of pure halcyon calm.

Now the late afternoon sun casts a glow over the freshly mown field, where guests move languidly in the space between the marquee and the river, smiling and embracing—the fine, bright air as sparkling as the champagne in their flutes. In this quiet country meadow, with the river running softly by, I feel as happy as I have ever been. As happy as I think it is possible to be.

Here is my friend Elizabeth—like me, looking older—but recognizably herself, a busy doctor, but also the girl I grew up with in steamy, river-saturated St. Louis. And here is Gail, my brainy competitor in college, who urged me to greater heights of ambition, but who also suffered the crises of early marriage and motherhood with me. And here is Julian, who knew the best wines and hosted the most elaborate dinner parties in graduate school—as warm, funny, and companionable as I remember him. Together, we create a complex web of experience: of marriage, divorce, career crises, children, and stepchildren. And loyalty to friendship through it all.

I wonder if this is what is meant by the idea, or fantasy, of resurrection. What we want most of all in our lives is to remain attached to the people we've loved. Yet, life whirls us apart. On those rare occasions that we come together again, we get a glimpse of what it might mean to be in paradise—surrounded by friends, lovers, spouses, parents, and children, regardless of the betrayals we commit or suffer over time—rejoicing now in each other's company.

Perhaps life's deepest desire—what Freud might have called Eros—is to gather and integrate our memories?

As it nears time for the toasts, I begin to wonder about the wisdom of the little reading from *The Tempest* I've proposed. Emma and Grace are both eager for it, and Lucy has given her blessing, but Jess seems uneasy. I overhear a whispered conversation between her and Jim at dinner. He thinks we should perform after the lead toast, offered by the father-of-the-bride, whereas Jess believes we should wait until after Jim and his best man speak. I'm sorry to be a source of contention, but it's too late to back out.

In my state of general euphoria, I may have misread my own daughter's wishes. The last thing I want is to create tension between her and Jim. When Jess turns to me, expressing her agitation, I remain silent, not wanting to add to the conflict. I leave the question of timing up to Jim, uncomfortably aware of the unorthodox nature of my request.

Jim rises on cue and takes the microphone from Frank. Graciously, he introduces me, Emma, and Grace, as if he had planned it this way all along.

The three of us step forward as Jim hands me the microphone. I thank him for allowing us to break with tradition. "But we're Americans," I say, "and somewhat impulsive. Though we're very sincere." Cheers and applause greet this statement. Everyone's in such a good mood that anything we do is all right.

Emboldened, I talk about Devil's Pulpit, the Druid site, and the spirits that surely haunt this ground—many of which must be female.

"At least I'm sure there's a local goddess of this field," I say, pausing and turning back toward the head table, "and her name is Diana."

Wilder cheers and applause.

Then I set the stage for Shakespeare's pageant.

"Before he gives up his magic powers," I remind the audience, "Prospero uses them one last time, to summon Iris, Ceres, and Juno to bless his daughter, Miranda, and her husband-to-be, Ferdinand. You have to imagine, for a moment, that we are goddesses—which is something of a stretch for me, though not for Emma and Grace.

Emma smiles at this, while Grace hides her expression by turning her head, swinging her hair in front of her face.

"I'll be Iris, Emma will be Ceres, and Grace will be Juno," I continue, as Emma hands me the text, holding the microphone steadily.

"Ceres, most bounteous lady . . . whose watery arch and messenger am I," I lead off.

In the video I see how uncertain I am, as Emma watches me, clear-eyed and confident.

"Hail, many-coloured messenger," she begins, with the ease and aplomb of a born actor, "why hath thy queen / Summon'd me hither to, this short-grassed green?"

"A contract of true love to celebrate," I reply, regaining my voice, "And some donation freely to estate / On the blesst lovers."

"How does my bounteous sister?" Grace chimes in. "Go with me / To bless this twain, that they may prosperous be, / And honour'd in their issue."

Do Grace and Emma know the meaning of "issue?" Perhaps not, but they have rehearsed their lines perfectly. And their dad has already alluded to the prospect of grandchildren, so they know what's at stake. Someday, they will be aunts, hopefully in the not-too-distant future.

In our rough stage-planning the day before, we were going to speak the last two parts together, but it falls out this way, instead.

Grace/Juno:

> Honour, riches, marriage-blessing,
> Long continuance, and increasing,

> Hourly joys be still upon you!
> Juno sings her blessings on you.

Emma/Ceres:

> Earth's increase, foison plenty,
> Barns and garners never empty:
> Vines, with clustering bunches growing;
> Plants with goodly burthen bowing;
> Spring come to you at the farthest
> In the very end of harvest!
> Scarcity and want shall shun you;
> Ceres's blessing so is on you.

Jessica's two half-sisters, still girls themselves, deliver the wedding blessing I've been carrying in my mother's heart.

If anyone fills the shoes of Ceres—the Roman goddess modeled on the Greek goddess Demeter, whose daughter was swept away from her by the underworld god Dis—it is me. A woman who is about to entrust her daughter to the care of a somewhat unknown man and an even more unpredictable future. I can't let her go, not without giving her a formal sign of my blessing.

Now that it's done, I feel relieved. As if a spell has been spoken, weaving its charm around the bridal pair.

As the light fades outside, a live rock band moves into the marquee, urging us onto the dance floor. A necklace of lights appears, suspended from the tent's central pole, causing the world outside to recede even further.

When I step out at last, the air feels refreshingly cool, but it is uniformly dark. We are in the country, where on a night like this you can see the moon and stars more clearly than your hand before your face.

I hear the river in the distance, but I cannot see it. Only the torches burning a path to its grassy edge articulate its presence—and danger—outlining its slippery margin for approximately fifty yards in either direction.

Here and there, I perceive a guest or two taking the air, illuminated briefly by the flare of a torch or the glowing end of a cigarette.

I linger, savoring the night air, the muted sounds of music emanating from the tent, and the shifting patterns of the dancers' bodies silhouetted against its sides, like figures in a child's magic lantern.

And then I see Jess—at the entrance to the marquee—in conversation with her dad. I walk over to them, hoping to share this intimate moment.

Jess, who has changed out of her bridal gown into the form-fitting, silvery dress that once belonged to my mother, is crying.

"It's just," she says between catches in her breath, "that you want the people you most love in your life to love each other."

I understand. She's talking about Frank's and my divorce. But why now? Why return to such a painful moment on the occasion of her own happiness?

"But we both love *you*," I say. "We always have."

I want to console her but am also feeling at a loss.

Frank reaches his arm around her as she tries to wipe her tears. I put one arm around her and one around him, and all at once we are all three embracing.

Frank's niece, Jamie, walks up, and we include her too. I'm standing too close to one of the torches, and another guest, seeing this, gently pulls me away.

Before Jess goes back into the tent, I ask her to pose for a photograph. I want an image of her wearing my mother's dress.

In it, she is smiling again—her slender form, strong cheekbones, and swept-back hair a reminiscence of my mother's young body, bloom, and promise. But it isn't so much my mother I'm thinking about. It's both of my parents in their early adulthood and their hopes for the future.

Neither could rise from their graves to attend this flawed but perfect wedding. Yet, I feel that they are here—in the dress that embodies my image of the life they once lived and the love they felt for each other.

All of a sudden, I understand my surge of emotion on first seeing Jess model my mother's evening gown. In it, she links the vanished past with the fleeting present, bearing both— like the mists now rising and obscuring the banks of the Wye river—into the flume of the future.

For a moment, I picture us all joining hands—the dead, living, and as-yet-unborn—in serious, ghostly dance.

Then I walk back into the tent.

Bountiful

Café Paradiso

Mr. Ramsay, stumbling along a passage one dark morning,
stretched his arms out, but Mrs. Ramsay, having died rather
suddenly the night before, his arms, though stretched out,
remained empty.
　　　—Virginia Woolf, *To the Lighthouse*

At the end of the summer of 2002, I fly from Minneapolis to
Granbury, Texas, for my ex-husband's family reunion, a
sprawling, bi-annual affair, which I haven't attended since our
early married days—a lapse of thirty years. Jess has been urging me to come, assuring me that everyone wants to see me.

"Really," she says, "they ask about you. Marilyn's husband,
Pete, even says I remind him of you."

I look at her closely. With her wavy, amber-colored hair,
high cheekbones, and wide-set medium-brown eyes, she
could be a professional model. She's even done some work
along these lines. At the height of her modeling phase, she
posed for an airline ad—a deep irony, given her long-standing
fear of flying.

In it, her hair curls in soft tendrils around her face as she
gazes calmly at the viewer, a trace of a smile on her lips—a

cross between Sandro Botticelli's *Venus* and Leonardo da Vinci's *Mona Lisa,* with a hint of one of Fra Angelico's serene Madonnas in the background. Her image was used for a short period of time in publications aimed at first-class passengers. The caption reads, "I wonder if this is perfect freedom?"

The reunion is scheduled for the Labor Day weekend, always a difficult time for me, as it was just before Labor Day that my dad died. Better for me to be with other people than alone at this time of year. Also, it's Nellie May's ninetieth birthday celebration. Since I've been visiting her in recent years, I want to be there. I may even get a chance to view the long-awaited video of Jess's wedding in June. I book my ticket to Dallas/Fort Worth, reserve a room at the resort lodge where everyone is staying, and arrange for transport from the airport.

The lodge, which overlooks a small (by Minnesota standards), yet pretty lake, is a bit run-down. It's a useful location, Jess tells me, for the scattered Texas clan, and the family has been gathering there for many years. Despite the faint, musty smell when I open the door to my suite, I find compensations—a bedroom separate from the living area, a fully equipped kitchen, and a sitting room that opens onto a balcony with an unobstructed view of the water.

The first thing I do, after setting down my suitcase, is open the sliding door to the balcony, push back the screen, and step out into the air. Being near water, especially the unruffled surface of this small lake, makes me feel at ease, even contemplative. My impulse is to bow down in prayer.

My room is adjacent to Jess and Jim's, whom I haven't seen since their wedding. They haven't yet arrived. I unpack my things, take a nap, and wake to a bustle of activity next door. When I've dressed, redone my make-up, and smoothed my hair, which has gotten thick and springy in the 98% humidity, I knock on their door.

Jess, looking fresh in a sleeveless top and light cotton skirt, invites me in. She's already laid out chips and dip and has opened a chilled bottle of wine. Jim's still in the shower. I'm glad to have some quiet time before greeting Frank's family, most of whom I haven't seen since my early thirties.

After the wedding, I felt a let-down, all the more disappointing given my state of euphoria in the weeks, even months, preceding it. Nothing had prepared me for the realization that when it was all over Jess would go away—that I'd feel her absence as acute pain.

I was like Demeter, suddenly perceiving that her daughter was no longer chatting amiably by her side, but rapt into another world, where she could not follow.

"You're suffering daughter-loss," my therapist reminded me gently when I described my symptoms.

She's right, I thought. But what if this condition is permanent?

Seeing Jess—looking like her normal, pre-wedding self—I feel reassured. She hasn't vanished forever.

There's a potluck supper this evening in the recreation room, each family bringing food for themselves and something to share. But, before this, Jess, Jim, and I go to her grandmother's room, where she has been settling in with the help of her caregiver, Trish.

Nellie May's room also faces the water—though it's on the ground floor and accessible to anyone who passes by. One by one, family members drop in to greet her and congratulate her on her ninetieth birthday. In her wheelchair, with one arm slightly bent from a mild stroke some years ago, Nellie May welcomes everyone. She's the unassuming matriarch of the family, the still center of its turning world. As part of her entourage, I am accepted without question—a quirky, prodigal daughter who has finally come home.

At dinner, I seat myself next to Frank's sister, Marilyn, and her husband, Pete. As we scoop up mouthfuls of potato salad, fruit compote, fried chicken, white bread, and barbecue, we talk about family—about Jess and Jim's wedding, which

Marilyn and Pete couldn't attend, and the deaths that have occurred over the past year.

Nellie May has lost two of her siblings: her sister, Elsie (who had succumbed to Alzheimer's some years before), and her half-brother, Harry, the son of her father's first wife. Harry was married to Carolyn, a small, bird-like woman, now in her mid-nineties, who looks pretty much the way I remember her. Everyone says she's ageless, and I believe this when I see her. "It's so good to see you," she says, as if we'd parted only yesterday, opening her wiry arms to embrace me and giving me a quick peck on each cheek.

No question about it, though, Nellie May's generation is waning. She's nearly the sole survivor of her original family system. Her parents, along with most of their progeny— Nellie May's three half-brothers, full brother, and younger sister—have now gone. Only she and her older half-sister, Margaret, remain.

No one seems surprised by my presence—especially the younger members who were children when Frank and I divorced—and I'm glad to blend in. I came here mainly to avoid being alone on the anniversary of my father's death, but something more important is happening. I'm taking up a place I once ceded in a dense family system, not without its own disappointments and losses, but which manages to carry on. Perhaps this is why I chose Frank in the first place— not because I knew how to love, but because I wanted more family. I'm like a fish that cannot thrive alone in an aquarium, needing a school to swim in.

After dinner, people begin to drift outside, drawn by the flash of late sun on the mirror-smooth surface of the water, wanting to light a cigarette (these are the younger ones), or just seeking a breath of fresh air. I move from one group to another, saying hello, pausing for a moment's conversation, then walking a few steps to greet someone new.

Suddenly, I realize I've entered one of those odd, dream-like spaces that Wordsworth writes about. There's nothing out of the ordinary, but I see everyone moving in slow-motion, our bodies languid, our voices muted, in a delicately shifting relationship to one another that seems random, but also appears—in a slurry kind of after-image—beautiful and inevitable.

Could it be that our lives are set to a tempo—a kind of internal dance, like the echo of our mother's heartbeat in utero—that we only faintly detect as we grow older? Or perhaps we become more appreciative, as we age, of moments of such quiet pleasure as this—when nothing is happening other than the steady beat of time and our silent enfolding within it.

Flash freeze.

The next night, at Nellie May's ninetieth birthday celebration dinner—in the same recreation room as the night before—my photographer ex-husband takes the ritual reunion photograph.

Back in the '70s, when we were married, I remember being annoyed with his elaborate preparations—the choice of location, the arrangement of seating (oldest and youngest in front, with the other rows based on height), the setting of the tripod and timer, the focusing of the lens. No wonder we got so fidgety—some feeling stiffness in their joints, others getting impatient, babies beginning to cry, and those still small enough to feel no embarrassment breaking away to be enticed back.

This time, I don't care how long it takes. Earlier in the evening, I looked through an album of reunions such as this—with photos covering thirty years. Except for the first of these, I am absent.

But there in 1972, when Frank began to document these gatherings, I find myself—twenty pounds lighter, with long, carefully straightened hair—standing in the last row, with the taller, and mostly male, members of the family.

And no matter how much Frank fusses over his lenses and angles, I'll stand here, shifting from one foot to another and smiling. I want to be a part of this history, this family. Now.

ॐ

Earlier in the summer, after Jess's wedding at the beginning of June, I flew to Italy for a literature conference in Arezzo, feeling a little silly about making two transatlantic trips in one summer but also not having the energy to plan for six weeks of continuous travel in Europe. As a result, I hardly had a room reserved and my ticket bought by the time I left. My trusty agent, Tim, booked me on a flight through London to Pisa, where he assured me I could get a train to Arezzo without any trouble. Glad to avoid Rome and the confusion of schedules I remembered from my trip to Spoleto six years before, I happily adopted this plan, which worked even better than I imagined.

After practicing my request for *un biglietto per Arezzo* in my primitive Italian, I approached the agent's booth in Pisa—conveniently situated in the airport itself—and discovered that a train was leaving within half an hour for Florence, where I would change trains to Arezzo.

Once I'd found my connection in Florence, I sat back with relief. All the transitions of travel make me uncomfortable. It doesn't matter how practiced I am, something about the moment of suspension between getting off a plane and finding a train, subway, or cab to my final destination makes me anxious.

It's as if I'm reliving the awful period of uncertainty after we left the isolated riverbank on the Mississippi where my dad disappeared.

How would he—or any of us—ever get home?

Behavioral therapists say it's best to deal with a phobia head-on. To identify the irrational fear, track it to its source, break it down into manageable bits of experience, and then practice confronting it. Anyone looking at my life from the outside might say I'd done this.

Driving, for instance, no longer terrifies me; in fact, I now love to drive, in part because I can get myself from one place to another without having to move from one mode of transportation to another, thus avoiding the uncertainty of transition.

And I fly more frequently than most. Yet, I still feel a churning in my gut while preparing for a trip and don't feel quite safe until I've actually arrived—and then returned home.

I go away and return—over and over again—in a pattern Freud would have understood as repetition compulsion. In his essay "Beyond the Pleasure Principle," he describes a game he observed his favorite grandson playing—throwing a spool out of his crib and then pulling it back again, saying something like *fort-da*, "gone" and "here again." The boy's father, Freud tells us, was at that moment in time actually away at the front. Though the child's father survived the horrors of World War I, his mother (Freud's first and most-loved daughter) died in the influenza epidemic that ensued. The boy died not long afterward.

From the experience of his own losses, Freud constructed a new theory—that of the "death instinct," which claims that what each of us desires most at heart is to return to the state of undifferentiated being that precedes our birth. There are times when I can understand this—when the effort it takes to get through an ordinary day is so daunting in prospect that all I want to do is go back to sleep. Yet, something also summons me to travel.

On the last leg of my trip from Pisa to Arezzo, I have an intimation of what draws me on. The train I've taken—which I'd thought to be the express—moves so slowly and stops so frequently I feel sure it must be the local. I'm so tired, however, that I don't care.

The seats are covered with dust, and the windows, one of which I pry open with difficulty, are exceptionally grimy. Yet, as the train slowly ascends, swaying gently from side to side, I find myself falling into a dream-like state. I note each passing station, concerned not to miss my stop, but I also feel as though nothing very much matters—as if my destination (however distant, unpredictable, or unexpected) is benign.

As I draw closer to Arezzo—where I feel I may never actually arrive—the air begins to feel fresh and cool. We are climbing out of the flat, sheet-metal heat of the plain. If my trip consists of nothing more than this—the dirty seats and windows of my second-class car, the silent travelers arriving and exiting, and the clicking sound of the wheels on the rails—I will be happy. Perhaps this Twilight Zone train is even taking me into the afterlife—like that TV episode I remember from my childhood, where a busload of passengers in the mountains slowly realizes they've all died and are on another kind of journey.

This one ends in the usual way. I get off in Arezzo and find a taxi to my hotel—to which the driver takes a circuitous route in order to disguise the fact that it's within walking distance, thus earning a higher fare while also saving me the embarrassment of my ignorance. I check into a comfortably air-conditioned room, take a quick nap, shower, and wake to a violet-colored light emanating from the narrow, full-length windows that open out to the street and the faint noise of traffic rising from the nearby piazza.

⁂

The morning after the first evening in Granbury, I accompany Jess and Jim to Nellie May's room, where she continues to greet latecomers. I give her the gift I've prepared for her birthday—an album of snapshots of the wedding. As it happens, I'm one of the few who took photos before the actual day of the ceremony. As a result, she can see, in time-lapse stages, how the week unfolded up to the wedding and for a few hours after. The video will supply the rest.

I show her the path from my B&B to Di's place in Brockweir; the arrival of Frank, Lucy, Emma, and Grace; the croquet game on the upper terrace; the clouds hanging low over the marquee in the soggy field; the evidence of the dogs' attack on the cake; and Jess looking slim and elegant, smiling through her tears in my mother's slinky, 1940s dress. Standing next to Nellie May, flexing my knees to be closer to her height, I tell her the story that accompanies each photograph.

I have no presentiment—as I offer this gift—that this is the last time I will see her.

≈

In Arezzo, I wake to a clear, bright morning. Like Spoleto, this town is small, with streets leading steadily upward to a central plaza embraced by many beautiful buildings, some civil, some religious. I spend the morning with a friend from the conference, walking up the *corso* to the cathedral where a series of frescoes by Piero della Francesca, having been recently restored, are now on view.

I know of Piero's work slightly and in a mediated way—through a haunting film titled *Nostalghia* by Andrei Tarkovsky. A master of the Soviet cinema, Tarkovsky made this film in Italy during a period of self-imposed exile. Already ill with the cancer that would end his life, he weaves a tale of alienation, sacrifice, and (secular) redemption against a shifting Italian landscape—which includes a pilgrimage to the site of one of Piero's most beautiful and enigmatic frescoes, a depiction of the pregnant Virgin Mary, referred to as the *Madonna del Parto*.

This painting, which has been moved from its original location in the apse of the church of Santa Maria di Momentana in Monterchi and restored more than once, now resides in a former elementary school building, where I view it up close at the end of my conference. But my impression of Piero della Francesca had already been formed by Tarkovsky's slow, reverent, cinematic approach.

In *Nostalghia*, a young woman guides the central male character to the church in Monterchi to view the fresco, but at the last minute he declines to leave the car. She enters the cathedral alone, where she gazes at the figure of the Madonna, whose eyes are dreamily half-closed, her sensuous mouth curved in a faint pout, and her blue gown discreet, capacious and wide, but parted suggestively from the neckline to the crotch.

To add to the ambiguity of the image, the Virgin's right hand is poised at the level of her abdomen, her forefinger delicately opening the gap in her gown to reveal the white cloth underneath. Beside her stand two angels, distinctly smaller in stature, holding aside a heavy curtain to reveal the figure of the Madonna, center-stage. It's as if they are replicating the gesture of the Virgin herself, calling attention to the center of her body—the locus of her sexuality and the invisible activity of her womb.

So identified was this image with fertility, and sacred to the local community, that there was public resistance to its removal from its original chapel setting and even more resistance to its being lent to an exhibition in Florence—for fear that mishaps in childbirth might result.

In Tarkovksy's film, the image of the Madonna—opening herself, as it were, to the eyes of the viewer—seems to represent some fantasy or possibility of acceptance and reconciliation. When I see her myself, I feel entranced. She's sexy, but also sedate—a fifteenth-century version of sacred pornography. A woman who is opening and touching herself before our eyes, while fully in command of herself and her situation.

ॐॐ

After the reunion, I talk with Jess on the phone about returning to Texas to visit her grandmother. We did get to show the wedding video but haven't really had time to catch up. On the other hand, we've just seen her, so we delay.

This conversation repeats itself over several months until Jess calls to tell me that Nellie May has been hospitalized for one of the myriad complications of her heart condition. Remembering how my mother's health declined precipitously in her final year—with edema and shortness of breath leading to increasingly frequent hospital visits—I feel a shiver of concern.

Jess calls every few days with updates on Nellie May's progress. At last, she is released from the hospital. We reassure each other with this news. Jess has a wedding of her friend Alex from high school—to attend in Spain, and I'm committed to a conference at about the same time. Afterwards, we agree, we will make arrangements to see her grandmother.

I come home one Friday evening to an urgent phone message.

"This is Frank," the speaker says, his voice faint and obscured by background noise, the kind I've learned to associate with airports. "I'm on my way to Texas. I'll call you from there."

Almost without thinking, I dial Nellie May's number in Wichita Falls. Frank's sister, Marilyn, picks up the phone.

"Mother is fading fast," she says, with her usual simplicity and candor.

"Would it help you for me to come?" I say, realizing instantly how useless my offer may sound.

"If you can come, we'll be glad to have you."

"I'll try to reach Jess first," I respond, suddenly aware of how vulnerable my daughter is—an ocean and a continent away.

But how will I contact her? I don't have the details of her itinerary or know where she's staying, except that it's somewhere in the vicinity of Bilbao. My super-organized daughter, who is much more in command of her schedule than I am of mine, has neglected to provide this crucial information.

Later, around 11:00 p.m. that evening, Frank calls back.

"Mother passed away sometime around eight," he says.

"Did you get there in time?"

"With an hour to spare."

"Were you with her?"

"We all were—Marilyn and Bob and me." He hesitates and then goes on. "Do you know what her last words were?"

"Tell me."

"She asked for some water, and I gave her a sip. She said 'thank you.'"

"That sounds like your mother," I say, straining to keep my voice even. "I'm so sorry. I loved her too."

"I know you did."

We are both silent for a moment—one we never imagined in our late twenties and early thirties when we fell so recklessly in and out of love.

"We have to reach Jessica," I say finally. "You can't have a funeral without her. She'll never forgive us if she isn't there. Why don't I take charge of this? And then I'll get back to you."

"OK," says Frank. "There's a lot to do here. I'd appreciate that."

The next morning I begin my search. I start with Christie, Jess's closest friend in New York. Because Christie shared Jess's 9/11 experience—and co-produced her wedding—I feel a special bond with her, almost as if she is my adopted daughter. Together, we strategize.

Christie will call Ivy, another good friend in New York, and Eric, with whom Jess has been developing a script for a film project. I will call her friends Hildur and Mariam, both of whom Jess has known since high school, who live in Minneapolis, and may (or may not) be at the wedding in Spain.

Later, we compare notes.

Neither Eric nor Ivy knows Jess's itinerary, and I haven't been able to reach either of Jess's Minneapolis friends, though I've left messages.

"How about Jim's mother?" Christie suggests. "Isn't Jim going to visit her after the wedding?"

"Good idea," I say and leave another message in Britain.

Finally Mariam calls me back.

"We couldn't go to the wedding," she says, "but I've got contact information in Spain. I know where Hildur is staying, and I've also got Alex's mother-in-law's number."

I call Christie right away, and she offers to call Hildur's hotel in Bilbao. By now, it's late in the day there, so I suggest that we wait. No one wants to hear about a death on the eve of a nuptial—hardly the groom's mother, much less the bride. We can resume this quest in the morning.

Di calls me back on Sunday. She doesn't know how to

reach Jess or Jim in Spain, though Jim plans to visit her afterwards. Jess will return to the States on Monday.

"Don't worry," I say, "I think we've found a way to reach her."

Then I call Frank.

"Here's Alex's mother-in-law's number," I tell him, "but I didn't want to call her on the eve of her son's wedding."

"Thanks," he says. "The girls and Lucy have now arrived, and Lucy speaks Spanish. She can make the call."

"Let me know when you reach her," I say, "and I'll make arrangements for us both to come to Texas. She's planning on returning to New York on Monday. I'll call my agent and see what he can arrange. Just remember you can't have the funeral before she gets there."

We're an odd team—a pastiche of friends, in-laws, current and former spouses—but somehow it works.

Lucy delivers the core message to the bride's mother-in-law the morning after the wedding. Alex, in turn, conveys this news to Jess, who calls her dad in Texas, who calls me, giving me Jess's hotel number in Spain.

When I get through to her, she's in tears.

But I'm on a mission. I now know the schedule. There will be a visitation at the funeral home on Tuesday afternoon and a church service on Wednesday morning.

"I'll call Tim," I tell her. "Just get home, and let me know when you arrive. I'll have something figured out."

❧

In Arezzo, I agree, one evening, to have dinner with a man I once loved. We're both English professors who spent a couple of months in the late '70s thinking we might make a couple. In those days, at the height of our youth, anything seemed possible.

Something ignited—and something didn't. At the apex of my passion, I wrote an erotic essay dedicated to him, detailing and delectating the pleasures I felt. I called it "Kingdoms are

Clay," after Antony's passionate outburst in Shakespeare's play *Antony and Cleopatra*, in which Antony affirms the supremacy of love over other human endeavors. "Let Rome in Tiber melt," he declaims, "and the wide arch of the ranged empire fall! Here is my space / Kingdoms are clay: our dungy earth alike / Feeds beast as man; the nobleness of life / Is to do thus."

"Make love not war," is what Antony is saying—a message my civil-rights, Vietnam War, sexual and women's liberation generation was particularly attuned to. Plus, we women had ready access to contraception—and no fear of STDs, a specter that would haunt the 1980s and beyond. For a brief, heady moment, we were free to pursue our impulses—choosing our partners, male or female, and having fun.

Those were the years in which I joined women's consciousness-raising groups, considered becoming a lesbian (though I'd never fallen in love with a woman), and went to bed with a man I liked because it seemed as good a way as any to get acquainted.

Now, I'm more thoughtful.

Yet, I'm glad for the opportunity to have dinner with someone I once loved—to share notes about our progress into late middle-age and to have a quiet, possibly even intimate, conversation. As I grow older, I'm aware of how much I treasure anyone who shares a morsel of my past. It's my friends who remind me of my history—who help me remember who I am.

On a breezy, quiet, late summer evening in July, my friend and I walk up the corso to the main piazza, where we choose a restaurant in the loggia that curves part-way around this space, like an arm laid lazily on the back of a convertible car seat.

Here, we share notes about our histories.

He's married—for the third time—and a grandfather. I'm twice divorced and single. He talks about his third wife and how he no longer responds to random sexual invitations. I look at him—lean, muscular, and handsome—and smile.

"I've got photographs of my daughter's wedding," I say. "Would you like to see them?"

Years ago, our daughters met at his home in his city. He bends over my photos, as we murmur over our daughters' current lives and interests. Later, another friend of mine at the conference tells me that he saw us, waved, and called, but we seemed oblivious.

ॐ∾

Tim works overtime to find me matching flights. By email, he sends me confirmation of two tickets—one from New York, the other from Minneapolis—to Dallas/Fort Worth, where Jess and I will meet to take a joint commuter flight to Wichita Falls. We'll get there in plenty of time for the visitation.

But this journey is not yet over.

When I arrive at the airport in Minneapolis, I get an urgent cell phone call from Jess. She's at JFK, where two flights have already been cancelled. Something is wrong with both planes.

"Look," I say, "tell them that your grandmother has died and you have to get to her funeral on time. Push your way to the head of the line." In the meantime, I go to the ticket agent at my own terminal and tell him my story. "Is there anything you can do to help?"

He tells me there's another flight from New York in about forty-five minutes but that it won't get to Dallas in time for our connection. No matter. I call Jess back. "See if you can make this flight," I say. "I'll go to the commuter terminal and wait for you there. If you don't get there in time, I won't board the plane. We can rent a car and drive to Wichita Falls."

Once I arrive in Dallas, I realize how unlikely it is that Jess will arrive in time. I have to get on a train to another terminal, then board a bus to the commuter flight location, a process that takes at least forty-five minutes. No way she can make it.

Just before my flight is scheduled to depart, the woman at the desk (to whom I've confided my dilemma) calls my name.

"We've just heard that your daughter's plane arrived forty-five minutes ahead of time. She should make it here before your flight is scheduled to depart."

How could this be? Jess has been bumped from two planes, leaving more than an hour behind her original schedule. Yet, I see her walking towards me from the end of the terminal, just as the boarding announcement begins.

"Your grandmother," I say, as I reach my arms out to her, "must have had a hand in this. Maybe she puffed out her cheeks and blew your plane forward."

৵৽

In Arezzo one evening, I attend a performance of Gabriel Fauré's *Requiem* in the local cathedral. It's open to all and free. I walk there with several friends from my conference after a convivial meal under the beautiful loggia in the main piazza. I've never heard this particular piece of music but am partial to the requiem as an expression of the sadness I've carried with me since childhood.

Death, by now, is familiar to me, something like a friend from grade school—one that I trust more implicitly than the more volatile and unpredictable lovers I've known, who promised a happiness that proved ephemeral.

My friends and I arrive with time to spare and settle ourselves on the folding wooden chairs ranged in front of the transept and altar. Italians are voluble, and there is much conversation around us—which continues at a high pitch until I begin to feel restless. At last, the orchestra and choir emerge. But then there's a long speech by the conductor that goes on for another twenty minutes or so. I assume he's elucidating the beauties of the score. Only later do I learn that this performance is dedicated to his predecessor, who has recently died.

This is a real requiem, sung for an actual person—like the ones I remember singing with my grade school classmates in St. Louis for deceased parishioners.

Once the music begins, I am entranced. Though somber, the mood also feels light. When the chorus sings the "Sanctus" I notice this quality more acutely. There is a kind of suppressed joy in this part of the music, corresponding to the moment that precedes the consecration of the Eucharist. The singers' voices rise, like helium-filled balloons, effortlessly ascending.

At the end, as their voices lift again, *"In paradisum,"* I sense a lightness within, gradually expanding into a state of euphoria, in which I feel a camaraderie with everyone I've ever loved. Borne aloft by the clear soprano voices of the singers, I feel myself ascending with them into an ecstasy of recognition and reunion.

Much later, I learn that Fauré had violated the order of the requiem, which emphasizes the painfulness of death and judgment—*dies irae*, the day of wrath and all that—by inserting this section, which belongs to an altogether different service. It took a special dispensation from the Church for his *Requiem* to be sung at his own funeral Mass.

But to me, the phrase "in paradisum" is familiar and comforting. I remember singing it as a girl in my neighborhood church for deceased members of our parish. In my childish mind, I had (like Fauré) merged it into my memory of the requiem.

ॐ∽◌

In Texas, after Nellie May's death, I find myself surrounded—and embraced—by Frank's family. Jess and I get there with just enough time to greet everyone and change our clothes for the visitation at the funeral home.

Together, we approach the small room crowded with flowers that contains her grandmother's body. We stand together, looking at her for a long while, as we start to cry.

"It wasn't real to me until now," Jess says, as we exit the room to speak to other relatives. Our progress is impeded by others entering, each of whom offers hugs and more tears. At last, we are in the vestibule.

"When I was with Nanny," Jess says, "I felt that everything would be all right."

I remember how irritated I used to feel when Nellie May would say "Everything works out for the best," which seemed like a cliché to me at the time—certainly not resonant with my own experience.

In my family, things tended to go from bad to worse. Knowing more about Nellie May's history of loss, I feel humbled. She put the best face on things she could—not out of naiveté but as a matter of disposition and choice. And she conveyed a sense of optimism and security to my daughter.

&⚬&

In Arrezo, there's a tiny café across the street from my hotel, which is especially popular in the evenings, as it hosts a full ice cream bar with a rainbow assortment of gelati—from the typical strawberry, chocolate, and vanilla through delicate shades of pistachio, butterscotch, almond, peach, apricot, raspberry, and mango. It's called Café Paradiso.

My hotel is at the foot of a steep hill, leading steadily upwards to the main piazza. Every day, as I climb this winding slope to view one of the town's historic sites, I pass this café—though I don't go in. With my map of the city in hand, I feel too purposeful to stop for coffee, much less gelato, which seems self-indulgent to me, before noon.

After a leisurely dinner with my long-ago lover, we descend the winding path—as slow and circuitous as a switchback trail in Yosemite—that leads back to the hotel. It's been a hot day, and it seems the entire town is strolling the streets with us, enjoying the somewhat cooler evening temperatures and the occasional puff of air. We are walking side by side in a companionable way, touching hands from time to time, but mostly not talking.

I turn to look at a lighted store display, featuring women's dresses. When I turn back, my friend is nowhere in sight.

I look down the street, thinking he must have strolled on. I can't find him. The flow of people—like a narrow, swiftly moving river—passes me in a sinuous current, while I am left standing mid-stream.

I look back up the hill, thinking he may have stopped also as I gradually outpaced him. No sign of him there.

For a moment, I entertain lurid fantasies. Perhaps he has literally disappeared—as in a film I once saw, in which a young woman is abducted at a car stop while her boyfriend naps on the grass outside.

This story, as I understood at the time, is an expression of my primal nightmare. It's called *The Vanishing*.

But how can anyone get lost in Arezzo? Even if I can't find my friend now, surely he will turn up later.

After standing still for several minutes—thinking he must be wondering about me too—I decide to join the flow of human traffic, slowly continuing my descent.

All at once I see him, walking uphill towards me.

"I turned around, and you were gone," he says.

"I looked away and couldn't find you."

I tell him about my fantasy.

"There's no bloodshed, no violence, no chainsaw gore, but it's the scariest movie I've ever seen."

"I know that movie," he says.

By now, we've reached the little park across from our hotel. The summer dark has descended, and the broad leaves of the sycamore trees make a soft, swaying sound in the breeze.

"Worst case scenario," I muse, "is that we'd meet again at the Café Paradiso."

"Not a bad idea," he says, following my gaze toward the ice cream parlor, whose warm interior casts a peach-colored glow onto the street. "I wouldn't mind a double scoop right now—maybe chocolate and raspberry vanilla."

"Or butter almond and pistachio."

Joining hands, we step off the curb and walk toward the café's beckoning light.

Bountiful

At times we think we know ourselves in time, when all we
know is a sequence of fixations in the spaces of the being's
stability—a being who does not want to melt away, and
who, even in the past, when he sets out in search of things
past, wants time to "suspend" its flight. In its countless
alveoli space contains compressed time. That is what
space is for.
            —Gaston Bachelard, *The Poetics of Space*

Once, when I was a child sick with rheumatic fever (for
the second or third time), confined to the small square of
my room and the even smaller rectangle of my bed, an occupational therapist who came every week, trying to interest or
amuse me with craft activities, asked me to name things I was
grateful for—in honor of the Thanksgiving holiday.

My mind went blank. As I saw it, my life had taken a bad
turn.

Embarrassed or annoyed by my silence, she began to
prompt me. "How about your family, your playmates, your
home, the food on your plate, honey?" she said, reaching into
her bag to show me the materials she'd brought that day.

I remember the awkwardness of our encounter, though
I don't remember her name, what she looked like, or how
my mother had acquired her services. I'd been shifted from

the private Catholic school I attended to the public school system to allow for at-home tutoring several times a week. Maybe the city provided for an occupational therapist as well? If not, my parents must have paid for her, realizing how hard it was for a seven- or nine-year-old to lie still in bed, hour after hour, day after day, for months at a time—the only treatment prescribed for rheumatic fever in the late 1940s.

I remember how she taught me to roll wet clay into tubes that I could lay one on top of the other, smoothing the sides with my fingers to make something in the shape of a bowl, which could then be glazed and fired. At least one of these lumpy things passed her approval, ending up as a container for pins, buttons, and loose change on my dresser. Another activity that kept me busy was winding bands of colored raffia around the form of a wastebasket, pressing each strand into place with white glue. My mother never threw this garish object away, moving it from the old house to the new one when I was a teenager.

But I don't remember anything else we did. Perhaps, sensing my lack of enthusiasm, my mother let her go. Or maybe the occupational therapist found a reason to discontinue her visits—finding me an odd child to work with, resistant and ungrateful.

The truth is I do not like to remember much of my childhood. First, I was sick (at ages seven and nine and convalescent in between), then my father died, and I was sick again at age eleven. The last time I was ill, no doubt in part from grief, my mother thought I might die—confessing her fear once I had begun to mend.

I shared her worry. At age eleven, I felt less thankful than ever. I was unable to remember the good things in my life— from my now long-ago childhood—without pain. What could the future hold but more suffering, more loss?

When I first had rheumatic fever, I had expressed a wish for a television. How I knew about this new technology when no one in our neighborhood owned one, I can't say. Maybe it was in the air—like gossip about the sleek new cars that suddenly appeared in driveways next to ours. One day, my dad came home with an RCA console model, which he placed in my bedroom, directly across from my bed. He liked new gadgets, and I think he would have bought one anyway, but the appearance of the new TV seemed like an answer to my prayer.

There wasn't much to watch at first. Most of the day, the TV just aired a test pattern. But then, around 5:00 pm, the monitor sprang to life. I remember watching *Kukla, Fran and Ollie*, a show with two puppets (Kukla and Ollie) and a live commentator (Fran), followed by John Cameron Swayze and the news. I didn't understand the wit of *Kukla, Fran and Ollie*, though I liked the puppets, and was distinctly bored by the news. But gradually, more programs were added. I loved *Howdy Doody*, a show that featured a hayseed puppet with a cowboy hat, freckles, and a toothy smile, and his life-size companion Buffalo Bob—a show more obviously geared toward kids.

My dad must have wanted to entertain me, as I remember friends of mine from the neighborhood being enticed to our house to watch the puppet shows in the late afternoon. But they were more intrigued by the life of the street, and many days I watched these programs alone.

There were also occasions when my parents took my two brothers to the river (where we kept our cabin cruiser) on weekends, leaving me with Nan, my maternal grandmother, to baby-sit me. She also liked TV, and we watched many programs that I doubt my parents would have approved had they been home. In this way, I viewed a lot of adult drama in the early years of television, when serious plays were performed before a live audience, with Nan, a rather reserved woman silently smoking in a rocking chair at my side.

Some of these programs scared me. One, I remember, was about a man tied to a chair in his basement with a bomb ticking next to him. Another was about a woman who hated her given name but only dreamed of calling herself "India" and escaping her dreary domestic routine.

Stories like these—unlike the movies I'd seen about cowboys and Indians, the Marx Brothers' antics, or the adventures of Francis the Talking Mule—seemed gritty and real to me. Their black-and-white tension, which lasted less than an hour, was interrupted by commercials for mundane objects like laundry soap or tires, but they held me spellbound.

Nan was not talkative, so I watched and listened, trying to fathom this strange new world of grown-ups. From what I could tell, it seemed filled with disappointment, a word I did not use to describe my own experience but whose flavor I recognized—like the smell of food that turned my stomach but which I had to eat anyway because it was good for me.

Sometime during the year of 1953—two years after my dad's death and the last time I was ill with rheumatic fever—I watched a play called *The Trip to Bountiful*. It had been composed especially for Goodyear Television Playhouse and was aired live, with all the flaws of a briefly rehearsed production. It starred Lillian Gish and (a very young) Eva Marie Saint and was written by Horton Foote—none of whose names meant anything to me.

Yet, something about this play remained with me more powerfully than any of the other dramas I saw at the time. It's about a woman in her sixties (then considered old and most likely the age of my grandmother who must have viewed it with me) who has one desire—to return to the rural Texas town where she grew up. A town named Bountiful.

I remember my grandmother, and I remember my room. My mother and two brothers do not figure in this scene. For one thing, we rarely watched television together. For another, there weren't enough chairs for us all in my bedroom. But my dad was already dead (drowned in 1951), so they couldn't have gone to the river. Perhaps they just went out.

Was I sick or just convalescing? The last time I was ill, I was confined to bed for six months, so I could have been in some phase of this slow journey toward recovery. With research and effort, I might be able to pin a date to this moment, but I don't think it matters. In my memory, it is just Nan and me absorbed in the unfolding of this story, mutely transfixed by the flickering black-and-white screen of the TV.

This is the story as I recalled it for years afterward.

An older woman is on a bus, where she strikes up a conversation with a younger woman in which they share intimate details of their lives. They arrive at a station, where the younger woman makes a connection to a different town. The older woman has left her purse on the bus, but it is found for her and returned. Somehow, in spite of many obstacles— including pursuit by her son, her daughter-in-law, and a local sheriff—the older woman arrives at her destination.

I didn't remember the beginning of the play, nor its end. What gripped me was the middle—the bus ride and the scene of the late-night bus station. I also remembered the intensity of the older woman's desire. She disliked her daughter-in-law and hated her life—cooped up in a tiny apartment with her distant son and his difficult wife. Yet, she knew what she needed—to return to her childhood home—and she was determined to get there.

In stark outline, this story seems painful. But I remembered it differently. Perhaps because of its title. Isn't "Bountiful" a good place to be? The old woman's journey was full of set-backs but also successful.

In *The Poetics of Space,* Gaston Bachelard muses on the complex meanings of the spaces we move through and inhabit, inventing a new word for this kind of activity: topoanalysis, which he describes as "the systematic psychological study of the sites of our intimate lives." He begins with the house, by which he means the first physical environment we experience, as we begin to awaken to the world outside our mother's womb.

I don't literally remember such a space, as we lived in the cottage where I was born until I was two, at which point we moved to the house where I spent most of my childhood.

The first cottage exists for me only in fragmentary stories and in photographs.

My mother has told me that I looked a lot, as an infant, like my older brother, which makes it hard for me now to know which (diaper-only) photographs are of him or of me. She has said that I was an active baby, learning to walk at barely nine months, loving to be outdoors, and getting out of my diapers when possible to run down the street.

The photos show little more.

In them, the house looks tiny and white (perhaps stucco?). There is a street in front, where our 1940s Chevy is parked; my mother, holding a baby (me or my brother?) is getting in or out. There is also a garden (perhaps in back of the house?) where my paternal grandfather, wearing a straw hat and an open-collar shirt, holds a diaper-clad baby lightly in his arms.

There is a handful of other photographs.

Most of these are set in a garden with a trellis covered with foliage. They capture my older brother and me in several poses. He is dressed in a plaid jacket, short pants, and Buster Brown shoes. I am wearing a white cotton batiste dress—what we now call handkerchief linen—and high top, white leather shoes, the kind that parents used to memorialize in bronze.

I don't really "own" these images, as they precede the onset of conscious memory, but they form a primitive visual narrative—this white cottage, this garden, this sequence of scenes—like a jumpy, silent movie that casts a dim glow over the background of my earliest standing-upright selfhood and curiosity about the world.

The house I grew up in—the one I remember—was a red-brick, three-story structure with a full basement and a finished attic where my maternal grandparents lived until my grandfather died. After that, Nan occupied this space by herself, a part of the family but also separate. She had her own stairway leading all the way from the kitchen to the third floor. When my dad died, she stayed with us, an occasional babysitter for us kids but a person somewhat remote.

My room was on the second floor, next to that of my two brothers. My parents' room was next to theirs, at the end of a horseshoe-shaped hallway. My room had one doorway adjoining my brothers' room and another opening into the central hallway. On one side of my bed there were two windows, giving me a view of the street. On the other side, there was a bureau and a clothes closet next to the hallway door. The color of the walls was a neutral beige, which I found boring. When, at last, we moved with my stepfather to a new house, I asked for eggshell blue. So much of my life (especially from age seven to eleven when I was ill) took place in this room that it is no wonder I remember it so clearly.

In the mid-1980s, I happened on *The Trip to Bountiful* again, this time as a feature-length film, aired on public television. The lead parts were played by Geraldine Page (who won an Oscar for best actress) and Rebecca De Mornay (in the Eva Marie Saint role). For all I knew, this was the same play I'd seen when I was eleven. Yet, everything about it felt different.

For one thing, the film was in color—a shocking transformation—and what I had remembered as the main action (on the bus and in the bus station) was framed by long opening and closing sequences.

I was in my mid-forties, married for the second time, and dividing the year between Minneapolis, where I taught at the University of Minnesota, and Berkeley, where I lived with my husband, who taught at the University of California.

I don't remember whether I viewed this film in Minnesota or California—alone, that is, or in company. What I do recall is my disappointment. Where Gish had seemed noble and even somewhat tragic to me, Page came across as manipulative and coy. De Mornay was sweet, but I couldn't help thinking of her as the heroine of *Risky Business*. Seeing this film again was like seeing too many replays of *It's a Wonderful Life*—a movie I'd loved when I first encountered it in childhood but which I grew to mistrust after its holiday commercialization.

Yet, some elements of the film version of *The Trip to Bountiful* managed to lodge themselves in my memory—enough for me to seek it out on video twenty years later.

My life altered in the interim. My second husband divorced me, my mother died, my daughter married, and I was now "Gramma" to a sturdy and mischievous one-year-old named Beatrice.

This time, I found myself intrigued by the opening and closing scenes, the parts I hadn't registered on my first viewing in 1953. I was acutely aware of the claustrophobia of the two-room apartment that Carrie Watts shares with her son, Ludie, and daughter-in-law, Jessie Mae. If one of them coughs, the others jump. No wonder that Carrie's restlessness and humming to herself in the first scene rouses first her son, then Jessie Mae, from sleep.

Carrie's desire to get away made sense to me. Travel, for her, means freedom. Once she's on the bus, she can relax. She can even confide in a stranger about how she married a man she didn't love, how she lost two children in infancy, and how her husband died, leaving her with a farm that slowly deteriorated, forcing her to sell and move to the city.

The middle section was more or less familiar to me. It was the ending that made me sit up and take notice.

In it, Carrie returns to the farmhouse where she was born, grew up, married, was widowed, and raised her son. The house is fallen down, of course—nothing like what she'd imagined. In addition, she learns that the childhood friend she'd hoped to visit has just died. She can go home, but she can't stay.

It's the sound of birds that I remember most clearly from this scene, along with Carrie's conversation with the sheriff who accompanies her to the old farmhouse and helps her to recall the bird species of the locale.

When I was little—no age I can pin down—I remember being awakened on summer mornings by birds chirping in an indiscriminate chorus outside my window. This, to me, signaled the long, leisurely, school-less days of summer, when I ran outside all day long, more or less unsupervised, with my friends from across the street and down the block.

Mothers, in this middle-class, post-war period of time, stayed at home—cleaning, doing laundry, preparing meals, and caring for pre-school-aged children. I never thought about such things when I was young. Instead, I enjoyed my freedom. To run out of our house (in the off-years when I wasn't sick) and call to my friends to play, an activity that occupied whole summer days, from breakfast to noon and after dinner, well into evening. This was followed by the insistent call from our mothers and the bedtime rituals of brushing our teeth, changing into pajamas (our bodies damp with sweat), and being read blissfully to sleep.

It was the sound of birds that revived this mélange of memories.

I'm not much of a naturalist, though I own books on geology, native trees, grasses and wildflowers, indigenous animals, and birds. I read them but don't worry over identifying anything, except by accident. Was that a rabbit or raccoon in my back-yard—or the elusive red fox that flashes through my compli-cated urban neighborhood?

So I can't tell you what birds sang me into wakefulness as a child in the shimmery, river-wet summer mornings of St. Louis. What I know is that this web of sound was like a reverse lullaby, a cheerful aubade, calling me into the thrilling promise of each new day.

Virginia Woolf once said that in her periods of madness she thought the birds outside her window were speaking to her in syllables (something like Greek) that she could comprehend. For her, the birds' voices were a harbinger of illness, a long, slow descent into a frightening realm from which she feared she would never return.

For me, birds (and their complicated social exchanges) are reassuring. I don't understand what they are saying, but I feel comforted by them. It's as if they perform an unrehearsed symphony each morning for anyone who listens. Even now, long before dawn, when I first hear them through my raised, screened windows in the upper Midwest city where I live, I feel calm, lighthearted, unreasonably happy.

How far back in time does this aural reminiscence extend? If I can't remember the cottage where I spent the first two years of my life, can I remember the babbling of birds? In my languageless state, perhaps this medley of sound mimicked the way I heard the adults around me, making sense without meaning.

Listening to my daughter as she was learning to speak, I marveled at how she would sing, sentence-like to herself, imitating the rhythms of speech without pausing over individual words. She was joining in the general medium of conversation without bothering with the drama of signification—as if she'd seen through it or gotten to the essence of communication—adding her own baby voice to the chorus of sound that made up her world.

Now, as I listen to my granddaughter, Beatrice, beginning the long journey from sing-song into speech, I can hear again the wobble between the impulse to play with sound for the pure pleasure of it and the wish to claim one's place and make one's mark on the world.

Some of her first words: "more," "up," "ba-ba," all expressions of need or desire. And then words for excitement, like "fwaa" for flower, "dog-dog," followed by an enthusiastic "arf-arf," a soft "burr" for bird, and one of her first and most pleasurable sounds, "duck."

Nearing two, she has learned the power of "yeah," accompanied by a nod of the head, and "no," followed by active or passive resistance. But she still loves to talk melodiously to herself—as if we can understand her as well as she understands us in our arduous explanations of why things are the way they are, why in particular she must get out of the swing right now, leave the playground, and come home. "No," she says, making clear that she's followed the ins and outs of our argument and come to her own conclusion.

In her stroller—when she will agree to be strapped into it—she will often fall into humming a version of "Old McDonald Had a Farm," mingled with "Twinkle, Twinkle, Little Star," as if the rocking movement over uneven sidewalk naturally induces song. It's borderline now, but soon the clear demarcations of individual words and syllables will win out over the musical rise and fall of run-on sound. Already, she is trying out primitive sentence constructions. "Iwantit," she says imperiously of a balloon, a toy, a piece of chocolate. Or "wheresdada," when her father has gone out for a run or a beer with his soccer-loving friends.

Yet, isn't language in its essence a distillation of song? Does music—in its myriad forms and diverse cultural manifestations—help to satisfy this need in adult life? Do we respond to it as we responded to the complex rhythmic and arrhythmic heartbeat of sound that rocked us in the womb and first welcomed us into life?

In the winter of 2006, I attended a staged performance of *The Trip to Bountiful* in an off-off Broadway production. I'd seen the ads and asked my daughter if she would arrange reservations while I was visiting. The play had enjoyed an extended run but was about to close. I didn't want to miss the opportunity to see it live.

This version of the play (developed from the original TV drama and the subsequent screenplay) opens with a hymn, sung from off-stage:

> Softly and tenderly Jesus is calling,
> calling for you and for me;
> see, on the portals he's waiting and watching,
> watching for you and for me.
> Come home, come home;
> Ye who are weary, come home:

Hymn singing, we learn in both the film and the play, is an irritant to Jessie Mae, who forbids it in the confines of the apartment. Once liberated from this hated restriction, Carrie breaks easily into song.

In Harrison, the first bus stop, she considers her luck in eluding her son and his wife, and in meeting the young woman, Thelma, who helps her locate the purse she left on the bus. "I seen Ludie and Jessie Mae," she says, "before they saw me. I hid out. Met a pretty friend like you. I lost my purse, and now I have somebody finding it for me. I guess the Lord is with me today," she continues, wondering also "why the Lord is not with us every day." Perhaps he is, she reflects, "and we don't know it." Unable to pursue this line of thought, she moves away from theological speculation—into song.

> Blessed assurance, Jesus is mine!
> O what a foretaste of glory divine!
> Heir of salvation, purchase of God,
> born of his Spirit, washed in his blood.

Turning to Thelma, she exclaims, "Oh isn't it nice to be able to sing a hymn when you want to," launching immediately into the refrain:

> This is my story, this is my song,
> Praising my Savior, all the day long:

Earlier, on the ride to Harrison, when Thelma confesses her fear for her husband, who is in the military and has been sent overseas (presumably to Korea), Carrie tries to comfort her. "Well," she counsels, "you just say the ninety-first Psalm over and over to yourself. It will be a bower of strength and protection for him. 'He that dwelleth in the secret place of the most High shall abide under the shadow of the Almighty. I will say of the Lord, He is my refuge and my fortress.'" At this, Thelma begins to cry. "If only I could learn not to worry," she says.

When I first read the Psalms in mid-life, I did not find them comforting. Rather, they seemed filled with anxiety and complaint. Enemies were everywhere, threatening destruction. God seemed more of a warrior than a protector, tipping the scales of victory in favor of the most urgent supplicant.

In the midst of this military rhetoric, I found it hard to hear the softer strains of gratitude or praise. Psalm twenty-three was an exception, but I didn't like to dwell on the Valley of the Shadow of Death, which I understood as a wasteland traversed not by the dead or dying, but by their survivors.

When I came back to the Psalms, it was by a circuitous route. I'd taken a trip to Death Valley—the California desert on the eastern side of the Sierras—and found myself haunted by words from the Protestant hymns we sang in morning chapel at the high school I'd attended in St. Louis. It was my stepfather who had sent me there against my then rigidly dogmatic Catholic faith.

Yet, the beautiful Protestant hymns—supplanting the iconography of the Medieval and Renaissance Catholic Church—entered me unawares. "A mighty fortress is our God, a bulwark never failing." "Oh God, our help in ages past, our hope for years to come." "A thousand ages in thy sight are like an evening gone." These elements of Hebrew Scripture, rendered into English and mediated by communal song, came back to me with energy and force.

In Death Valley, I was immersed in a landscape that resembles some of the desert terrain of the Middle East, the actual birthplace of the Psalms. Years later, when I visited the Negev Desert in Israel, I felt this resonance. Each has a stark beauty, full of subtle life and color that cannot be described— only invoked.

I loved Death Valley. Its stillness, seemingly unfiltered light from the sun reflecting back from the paleness of the ground, its sheltered feeling from the mountains rising up on each side, and the blue-violet-magenta play of light over these at sunset made me feel at ease. How could anything so impossibly beautiful be associated with death?

In the Negev, I felt the same. At Mizpah Ramon, I marveled at the expanse of desert and range, seemingly endless in all directions, its inhospitableness to human habitation protecting it also from human devastation.

On my last day in the Negev—to which I'd traveled with my physicist husband—I took a tour through the local canyon, guided by an organizer of the conference my husband was attending. What I remember now is the friendly, even domestic, nature of this walk—it was a sort of baby canyon, suitable for beginners—and the rich play of color along its walls.

We descended slowly down a trail to its heart, where we followed a small stream for a couple of miles. The sides of the canyon rose steadily above us—glowing pink, rose, salmon, and orange in the early morning light.

At last we came to a waterfall, descending from what seemed a great height and falling into a blue-green pool at our feet. Our guide had deliberately refrained from describing our destination. Now we stood in silence, surrounded by the warm, peachy-yellow walls of the canyon—like hands embracing us without touching—the water softly sifting from above and gathering into a basin that made me want to cast off my clothes and dive into it.

Instead, I gazed—speechless, like the rest of my group— at the steep canyon walls, the slow waterfall, the pooling waters, wishing that I would never have to leave. I was the only one aware that this was the morning of my fiftieth birthday.

What is it about desert that is so appealing?

There's dust, of course, from which we are made (or so we are told) and to which we return—the crumbly, gritty stuff of cremated remains or what survives of our bony infrastructure interred over centuries of time. But this wasn't what I thought or experienced in Death Valley or in the Negev. Rather, I was flooded with light.

What if place is not defined solely by physical spaces, like rooms or houses, but by the dimensions of sound or light? What kind of topoanalysis would this involve?

I'm not religious in any conventional sense, but I once had an experience that I might describe as mystical.

I'd been sitting quietly after a Sunday morning service at the Franciscan monastery I sometimes attend, when suddenly I felt a sensation of warmth and illumination. It was as if someone had flipped an interior light switch. This feeling was not uncomfortable. Rather, it felt ordinary and natural. It was just there—something like waking to the sound of birds—the difference being that my awareness of outside and inside had vanished, as if someone had opened a door or lifted the bars of a cage. I wasn't frightened by this transformation. Instead, I was pleased and curious.

I got up from my seat, walked to the entrance of the building, greeted my friends, and chatted with them, all the while aware of my unusual state of being. I was still myself, recognizable to others, and familiar with my environment. Yet, something subtle had changed.

This was nothing like taking drugs—speed, Valium, grass—all of which I'd experienced at one point or another in my life. I was completely myself, yet also not myself. I drove home in this curious state and then sat in my car in my own driveway, reluctant to do anything that might disturb whatever was happening. By now, I felt that I was in some kind of field of radiance—as if light were dancing through me into the grass, trees, and sky of my own front yard.

"If this is what it's like to die," I thought, "then it's all right."

Just as suddenly as this experience arrived, it left. Still sitting in my car, I felt that the light switch had been turned off. I didn't feel bad—as if coming down after a high—but rather that I'd returned to my ordinary way of being. I'd experienced something extraordinary—and then it was gone.

Was this some kind of weird brain event? Like the aura of a migraine, which some experience as a quasi-visionary state? I don't think so. I've had migraines, which I've never found illuminating, only painful. I didn't lose consciousness or enter any kind of ecstatic state. Neither did I lose my capacity to talk, drive, or find my way home. In every way I can describe, I was myself—yet radically open, as if all boundaries, everywhere, had been dissolved.

When it was over, I felt like something had happened, yet I didn't know what. There were no voices speaking to me from the clouds. No fiery fingers inscribing instructions in stone. I didn't even feel, like Virginia Woolf, that I understood the language of birds. What I had experienced wasn't about words or destiny. It was about light.

For a long time afterwards, I wished this experience would visit me again. I tried to imagine what I might have done to summon it and then to recreate those circumstances. For a while, I even believed that if it had occurred once that it must happen again. I tried to maintain a state of preparedness.

But whatever had happened was an anomaly. I can't get there again. If it's something odd about my brain chemistry, that circuit may have fired randomly but is now silent. I'm on my own again in the wildly unpredictable world.

When I viewed the stage play, I was especially attuned to its ending—with a conversation between Carrie and her son, Ludie, in which both reminisce about the old farm. Ludie confesses at this point that he remembers a summer night when his mother waked him to walk in the fields with her and enjoy the brilliance of a full moon—a memory he had earlier denied. They share other recollections, leading Carrie to comment on the cycles of time.

"You see," she says, "it's all woods now. But I expect someday people will come and cut down the trees and plant the cotton, and maybe even wear out the land again, and then their children will sell it and move to the cities, and trees will come up again." When Ludie affirms the possibility of such a scenario, she concludes, "We're part of all that. We left it, but we can never lose what it's given us."

Carrie's rather unexpected surrender of her fantasy of returning to Bountiful to live out her days leads to her equally surprising ability to negotiate with her daughter-in-law about the "house rules" Jessie Mae proposes. She even relinquishes her cherished Social Security check (which she had kept hidden from Jessie Mae's prying eyes). "It's all right, Son," she says, "I've had my trip."

But she asks for one last thing—to linger for a moment before returning to the car for the trip back to Houston. After sitting down in the grass by herself and putting her hands into the dirt, she rises and turns toward the house, saying, "Goodbye, Bountiful . . . goodbye." What follows is a voice-over reprise of the opening hymn: "Earnestly, tenderly, Jesus is calling, / Calling, O sinner, come home!"

The playhouse was small, and I was sitting closer to the stage than I ever had before. Jess, about six months pregnant with her second baby, was seated next to me, Jim to her left, and their friend, Fred (Beatrice's godfather), on the aisle. It hadn't occurred to me that the power of the production, my proximity to the stage, or the closeness of my companions might be especially moving. By the end of the play, I was fighting tears. As we got up to leave the theater, I was aware that all of us—Jim, Jess, and Fred, as well as me—were discreetly wiping our eyes. Over dinner, we talked about how the play had affected us. Jess commented on how accurate the accents of the actors were, reviving her memories of visiting her Texas grandmother and her dad's extended family when she was young. Jim recalled his childhood home on the banks of the Wye River—a property his mother had recently sold, as it had grown too much for her to tend by herself. Fred, whose background is Afro-Caribbean, remembered his mother, recently deceased, who resembled Carrie in her "old-fashioned" ways. Each of us had an interior "Bountiful," a beloved place to which none of us could physically return.

After seeing the stage revival of *The Trip to Bountiful*, I sought out the videotape of the original TV drama, which I located at the Museum of Television and Radio in New York City. Though performed live before the television camera in 1953, the play had been filmed in production and was now available in the museum's archive. All I had to do was submit a call slip, then wait at a booth with a display monitor for the tape to be delivered into my hands. At last I would see—or so I thought—what had so affected me at age eleven. Time travel was what I anticipated—the full frame-by-frame unfolding of the past, through the all-seeing lens of the camera. I sat forward in my darkened cubicle, turned the switch, and began to watch.

Lasting less than an hour, interrupted by commercials for Goodyear tires, the play was much shorter than the film and stage-play versions. It was also starker—partly an effect of the black and white contrast but also of the style of performance. Lillian Gish, who began her career as a silent-screen actress, played her role with none of the subtle humor or playfulness of Geraldine Page, but rather with an intensity that I associate with a silent film star's need to convey emotion through facial expression. Carrie Watts's story, as portrayed by Gish, was near tragic.

The first scene, in the Wattses' apartment, draws sharp lines of conflict between Carrie and Jessie Mae, who regards Carrie as something close to senile. Seizing her opportunity when Jessie Mae leaves for a beauty parlor appointment, Carrie flees. The play concentrates on the middle scenes—in the bus and the bus station—as I had remembered. The ending, when Carrie arrives at her old home, confronts her son with her need and loss, and departs with him and Jessie Mae, is dramatically distilled.

I was taken aback. What possible appeal could this story have had for me as a child?

Slowly, I began to see a resemblance between Carrie's dilemma and my own. Her cramped living quarters reminded me of my sick room as a child, while her querulousness and frustration mirrored my restlessness and boredom. Like Carrie, I imagined the past as a place I wanted to visit, a benign space where all my wishes would be granted—a place of bounty, full of blessing.

The weekend that I visited the Museum of Television and Radio, I stayed in my daughter and son-in-law's apartment by myself. Nearing the time in her second pregnancy when she would no longer be able to travel, Jess flew to California to visit a friend who had just had a baby, while Jim took Beatrice to see his father in Canada. With everyone away, I observed my environment closely. I'd always appreciated the apartment's high ceilings, tall windows, and abundant light. Now I began to look more carefully at the signs of Jess and Jim's family life, especially the photographs displayed in every room.

As children of divorce, Jess and Jim have parents, step-parents, and half-siblings in addition to the usual complement of grandparents, aunts, uncles, and cousins. As a result, there are many family photographs represented in the snapshots and formal photographs clustered on walls, bookshelves, and side tables. There are prints of all sizes and kinds—black and white, color, Polaroid—in frames both simple and elaborate. There are even a few—one, for instance, of my young mother sitting on a veranda in a wide-brimmed, black straw hat—stuck to the refrigerator with magnets. Empty of its inhabitants, the apartment is nonetheless populated with family members both alive and dead, rubbing shoulders with one another, unconstrained by time or necessity, bound only by the invisible force field of memory.

To save myself the trouble of unfolding the futon in the living room, I slept that weekend in Jess and Jim's bed. As a result, I woke each morning (as perhaps they do) to the sight of the photographs they've placed on their dresser bureaus. On Jim's side, there is a studio portrait of his mother, clear-eyed and smooth-skinned, her blonde hair loosely waved, the dimples in her cheeks barely discernible; an equally formal portrait of his father, looking grave and handsome in military uniform; and a commercial shot of his white-haired grandfather receiving an award for wartime service from a youthful Queen Elizabeth.

The photographs on Jess's side are more informal, consisting mostly of enlarged snapshots. In one, her dad and I are facing each other talking, each holding a drink, unaware of being observed. From the background and the style of my hair (long, straightened, the ends up-flipped), I'd say this photograph was taken in Texas and dates from the time of our engagement. A second photograph shows Frank, baby Jess, and me as a family during our first Christmas in Vermont. We are posed for Frank's camera—set on a tripod with a timer—wearing our holiday outfits. My hair, still long, is now pouffed up, while Frank sports a handlebar mustache. Jess, in a white cotton dress, straddles our laps, a look of happy surprise on her face. The last photograph, also taken in Vermont, in the kitchen of our country farmhouse, shows Jess at about nine months, on the verge of taking her first steps, holding onto my outstretched hands.

Seeing these photographs on either side of the room as I awoke each morning had a curious effect. It was as if my daughter and her husband had gathered their parents—divorced, remarried, living at a distance—around them in the only way possible, through their visual images. In this way, the families that had been broken, altered, and displaced reemerged whole. The photographs throughout the apartment, instead of memorializing isolated moments of the past, assembled them into something new—into a multi-faceted collage of their collective memories.

Ah, I thought, this is what Carrie seeks—not a literal return to the scene of her childhood and young adult happiness but a mind-space in which she can recall the important moments of her life, taking pleasure and sustenance from them.

And for me, at age eleven? I wonder if something in Carrie's story drew me forward into my as-yet-to-be-unfolded history. Toward an anticipation of the kind of bounty that might, one day, open my heart.

Angels and Dust

As a child I was always looking on rubbish heaps and in dustbins with a feeling of wonder. I like to think that, while in life things like pots and brushes and clothes etc. may cease to be used, they will in some way be reinstated, and in this Dustman picture I try to express something of this wish and need I feel for things to be restored.
—Stanley Spencer, The Tate Gallery Archive

On August 30, 2001, I am reading the final set of proofs for my memoir *Crying at the Movies*, which deals with my dad's drowning fifty years before. It is the anniversary of his death—to the day.

The weather in Minneapolis has been sweltering—well above 90 degrees, with close to 95 percent humidity. To make matters worse, neither my house nor my office at the university is air-conditioned. I can barely move, much less concentrate. I decide to drive to the North Shore, a wooded and rocky outcropping of land along the western edge of Lake Superior in Northern Minnesota, as it will surely be cooler there.

It takes about three hours to drive to Duluth, the port at the southern tip of Lake Superior, then about two more to reach the series of resorts that line the shore. Luckily, I've been able to book a room, last minute, at a resort that fronts the lake. All the rooms, I am told, face this dramatic body of water, which is so vast that it not only looks like an ocean but also behaves like one. A storm on Lake Superior can be as bad as any on the Atlantic.

The afternoon I arrive, the sky is alternately cloudy and clear. The sun is shining over the lake as I pull into the gravel parking lot of my lodge, but threatening clouds hang overhead.

True to the lodge-keeper's word, my room has full, clear views of the lake. Being on the second floor and at a corner section of the building with floor-to-ceiling windows, it gives the impression of being suspended in air—as if I can float out from my room onto the smooth surface of the water.

I unpack and go to dinner at a small, lakeside restaurant up the road. While I eat on the terrace, I watch the heavy clouds move swiftly over the water, trailing sheets of rain. In this light, the lake is steely blue.

By the time I get up to leave, the air has already begun to clear, though spatters of rain continue to dot my windshield on the short drive back to the lodge. Only when I get out of the car do I notice the effect of this change. The volatile combination of water and light has created a magnificent double rainbow, with one foot on shore, the other arced far out over the lake.

Never have I seen such a perfect rainbow—with no break in its shimmering bands of color—much less two at the same time, the second somewhat muted but equally perfect. The dominant rainbow is the lower one, its companion hovering slightly above. Both glimmer for well over an hour—red, orange, yellow, green, blue, indigo, and violet—the sky a giant prism. Even their dispersal is leisurely—a long, slow departure.

Guests at the lodge gather on the sloping lawn leading down to the ledges of rock at the shore, some reclining in Adirondack chairs, some standing with drinks in their hands, some fussing with their camera lenses, others pointing to the sky and exclaiming. Children run about, looking up from time to time, but mostly absorbed in their games. Random conversations spark among strangers. No one leaves until the last wisp of color fades.

I've come north for the most practical of reasons—to escape the heat and humidity and to read the proofs of my manuscript. Now, however, I become aware of another motive. I've also wanted to do something special—or at least different—on the anniversary of my dad's death. And look what I've lucked into: an apparition as magical as it is serendipitous.

Every day that weekend, I pore over the pages of my book, reliving the journey it describes—from the shock of my childhood loss, through the years of self-numbing, to the eruption of full adult grief. The book I've just completed has taken me fifty years to write. It seems fitting that I bring it to a close just now, at exactly this moment, in precisely this location.

The double rainbow feels like a blessing. At least that's how I choose to view it. I remember how my friend Margo interpreted the dramatic rise of the white bird out of the field as a message from her recently deceased mother. This manifestation lifted her depression, consoling her in her grief. Though skeptical of her conviction that the bird actually *was* her mother returning in spirit form, I can understand the efficacy of her belief. Now I find myself appreciating the strength of Margo's desire as I entertain the fantasy that the double rainbow is a message to me from my parents reunited in death. What better or more beautiful way to communicate?

Do I literally believe this? I'd have to say no. Yet, the synchronicity of events is compelling: the fiftieth anniversary of my dad's death, the completion of my book of mourning, and the appearance of the double rainbow. It's as if I have my parents' blessing or approval. As if I can now let go of the painfulness of my history without, however, forgetting it.

I'm reminded of a film I saw some years ago titled *After Life*, by the Japanese director Hirokazu Koreeda. The intriguing premise of this film is that after death we can choose one special memory to relive eternally. The film opens with a stream of deceased men and women arriving at a location (looking like an abandoned school building) where they are asked to select a single memory to carry with them into the afterlife. They have only a couple of days to make this choice. Then the memory will be recreated on film. After witnessing the screening of this film, the bearer of the memory will vanish into it.

One memory to live with for eternity—what a crazy idea! Yet, I couldn't help identifying with the characters in the film, scanning my own memories to see if I could select one that stands out as especially happy or gratifying. Quickly, I realized the impossibility of this task. Choosing a single memory— whether from my childhood, adolescence, middle years, or later life—will exclude all the others. Yet, the characters in the film seem to accept this challenge, and most are satisfied with the outcome. In fact, they are a remarkably cheerful group of dead people, easily charmed by the improvised film sets their interviewers (now turned amateur filmmakers) fashion to preserve their cherished memories.

Of course, there are exceptions. And here's where the film becomes really interesting. An elderly man named Ichiro Watanabe cannot come to a decision because his entire life strikes him as bland and uneventful. His interviewer, Takashi Mochizuki, a young man in his twenties, summons the video archive of Watanabe's life to prompt his memory. Gradually, the process of viewing his life on tape brings Watanabe to an awareness of how much he appreciated his uneventful, yet satisfying, arranged marriage. He is now able to choose—singling out a quiet moment between himself and his wife, sitting companionably on a park bench.

Suddenly the plot develops a new twist. It appears that the woman Watanabe married was Mochizuki's fiancée— Mochizuki having died shortly before the conclusion of World War II. Mochizuki realizes this connection while viewing the videotape of Watanabe courting his future wife.

Here we also learn something about the mysterious identity of the interviewers. They are neither angels nor messengers of God. Rather, they are people like their subjects—who could not, or would not, choose. Now our attention shifts to Mochizuki, who envies Watanabe for enjoying the life he himself had been deprived of.

To make matters even more complex, Mochizuki has a teenage girl assistant, Shiori Satonaka, who is in love with him. Shiori, perceiving Mochizuki's anguish over his lost life, helps him to locate the "memory film" of his former fiancée, now also deceased. It turns out that the moment she chose to immortalize was one that included Mochizuki—sitting with her on a park bench—not long before his death. Reassured, Mochizuki now seems poised to make his own memory choice.

But what has Shiori accomplished? Sensing that Mochizuki will leave her, she visits him in his room to express her regret at having helped him. Everyone abandons her, she professes bitterly. Not even Mochizuki will remember her, as all his previous memories will be erased once he's selected a single one to live with for eternity.

Once again the film takes an unexpected turn. Mochizuki's memory film will include his role as interviewer, as that is the experience he wants to preserve: the coming to awareness that his life had meaning for his lost fiancée. Because this moment of recognition came "after life," he can carry his afterlife with him into eternity.

Mochizuki's choice is unorthodox, and it requires special dispensation, but it also trumps the system. The memory that Mochizuki records on film is one of himself sitting on a park bench, musing on his experience of his life, which includes everything that has happened between him and his fellow interviewers, as well as his subject Watanabe.

After Life has a lighthearted feel to it, yet the plot shifts are confusing. I couldn't take it in on first viewing. It took several more screenings before I began to see that it might be more about memory than eternity.

Memories are powerfully important, the film seems to be saying—perhaps the only thing that most of us have to make sense of our lives—but they are not pure, nor do they render their meanings easily. Each individual memory in *After Life* is lovingly elicited, constructed, mediated, and then re-presented—on film. When pressed, Watanabe resorts to a videotape of his life to "remember" what mattered to him. Yet, we believe—at least I do—that the moment he chooses is somehow right. It doesn't seem to matter that the actual event on which his memory is based cannot be retrieved in original form. Rather, the "actual event" is a function of memory.

What we have, the film suggests, are memories of memories, something like a palimpsest, or an ongoing revision of a glimpse of something we dimly sense to have been important and whose fleeting significance we are still trying to capture and articulate—an image or script that we cannot resist altering or revising—until we die.

After Life offers an upbeat portrayal of the slippery, fallible, and malleable, yet also necessary, way that subjective memory works. Our memories are stamped as individually ours, yet they are also literally what we make of them. Out of such fragile material, we construct our life histories.

After Life deals with serious questions of memory and personal meaning with a playful, even comic, touch. We can walk away without feeling the need to ponder a deep message. Yet, much of what it has to say about how memory works parallels the evolving understanding of cognitive neuroscience, which posits personal memory as an ongoing narrative construction rather than a set of fixed references.

When we remember an event from our past, we do not simply submit a call slip to a conscientious librarian who will retrieve the desired item from a clearly marked storage location. Rather, what happens is more lively and unpredictable. A neural network "lights up," so to speak, in our brain, activating familiar pathways among neurons and their receptors. Yet, the point of stimulation—something happening in the present—is also entangled in this process. So what we "remember" is contaminated by new experience, new evidence. The "memory" we activate bonds, to some extent, with the circumstance of its recovery. As a result, the "memory" in question—through each successive activation—is altered.

What we remember is thus happening—and forever changing—in (and as a result of) the present. Memory, it appears, is a process rather than a product, a verb rather than a noun. In addition, it commingles past and present, which can no longer be understood as separate entities carefully segregated into different categories and locations in the brain, but rather inter-implicated, even colliding with each other, in ceaseless flux. Such a view may be counterintuitive, but it is also immensely intriguing.

If memory is unfixed and unstable, it can also be dynamic and integrative. Remembering is not simply nostalgic or regressive, as it is not a static activity. Rather, each act of recall participates, to some degree, in the flow of the moment. In this way, memory may function as a continuous process of integration—reanimating previous thoughts, feelings, and experiences to create a synthesis with ones that are in the process of unfolding. In this sense, one might say that moving backwards in time—though such "movement" is purely imaginary—is synonymous with moving forwards, which is to say living in the moment.

After Life represents something like this process. The film keeps revisiting different versions of Mochizuki's and Watanabe's past experiences while folding them into the drama of their interaction with each other. This interplay of memory and revelation leads to the comprehensive vision that Mochizuki achieves—in which his prior experience gains unexpected resonance and meaning. Mochizuki's memory film, by subsuming the past into the present, generates a new integration and imagination of his life history. It is this synthesis—this expanded awareness and body of memory—that he chooses to carry with him into eternity.

Something about Koreeda's film resonated with a shift in my own way of thinking about the past, which I had been used to regarding as too painful to dwell on. Now, instead of trying to insulate myself from my most difficult memories, walling them off or pushing them aside, I began to explore them. Much of this process coincided with the writing of *Crying at the Movies*, though I was not aware of it at the time. While I had anticipated some kind of therapeutic effect of completing this book—say, a lessening of anguish—I had not counted on a field change of awareness. I had not anticipated that I would begin to reconceive the relationship between my present and past experience. In particular, I had not imagined the degree to which the boundary between them would dissolve or the way they would begin to suffuse each other and interact.

In the individual mind (or brain), of course, there are no such boundaries. Yet, I had felt them, and that feeling had a determining effect. The subtle and gradually noticeable shift in my perception of this invisible dividing line also altered the way I experienced myself in time. In this curious way, changing my idea of the past not only changed my conception of time, but also changed *me*. Yet, how to articulate such a slippery awareness?

My sense of time and memory were undergoing major reorganization, yet I had no language for this new understanding. I found one in another visual form—this time in the work of the eccentric and somewhat obscure British painter Sir Stanley Spencer (1891-1959).

On a visit to the Bay Area in the late 1990s, I went to an exhibit of Spencer's paintings at the Palace of the Legion of Honor in San Francisco. I knew nothing about Spencer. It was just a beautiful day, and I went there with a friend on a lark.

I was immediately taken with Spencer's work, much of which portrays Biblical stories in terms of village life, borrowing local figures set in familiar surroundings to represent saints, apostles, the risen dead, and Christ himself. What captured my interest was the vividness and intensity of Spencer's vision—so materially real, yet also unearthly. I was also moved by the oddness and inclusiveness of his imagination—men and women make love with plants as well as animals in some paintings—along with his fascination with the theme of the Resurrection. To make matters even more complex, Spencer anticipated the hyperrealism of artists such as Lucien Freud in his series of nude portraits, where his subjects (including himself) are depicted with brutally loving honesty.

This exhibit was so overpowering that I couldn't quite take it in. I bought the catalogue and then put it aside until the year after my daughter's wedding, when I flew back to the UK to attend a literary conference outside of London. The Tate Modern holds a substantial number of Spencer's paintings, so I went to look at them, realizing also that Cookham-on-Thames, the place where Spencer was born and where he spent most of his life, was only a short train ride away.

On impulse I went there. I also took the recommended "Spencer Walk" past his childhood home and many of the landscapes depicted in his paintings. It was an unseasonably hot day for England. I strolled along the Thames, past the village churchyard—the scene of Spencer's magnificent *Resurrection* painting (1924-27), also the location of his unfinished *Christ Preaching at Cookham Regatta* (1952-59)—to the fields where Spencer felt his most intense visions or anticipations of heaven as a child.

Who was this guy? And why was I falling for him?

No question that Spencer's vision was odd, an amalgam of caricature, realism, Christian symbolism, and erotic obsession. Also, he seemed to want to include *everything* in his idea of the afterlife, not unlike Mochizuki's sly solution to the problem of memory selection in Koreeda's film *After Life*. I was now on a quest; I had to know more.

Spencer, I learned, was born into a somewhat nonconformist Victorian family. His father was a local music master, his mother a warm and evidently fertile woman who gave birth to ten children in all, Spencer being the eighth of those who survived. Religion was part of the very air Spencer breathed—his father was Episcopalian, his mother Methodist. Family dinners included lively debate and argument, the children expected to voice their own opinions. As a child, Spencer, despite his diminutive stature, was dubbed "Tiger" for his fierce temperament. He was, like his younger siblings, educated at home by his sister, Anne, who held classes in a garden shed—until he entered the Maidenhead Technical Institute at the age of sixteen. He later attended the Slade School of Art in London, though he commuted from home, earning him the nickname "Cookham" among his classmates.

There were two major turning points in Spencer's life. The first was The Great War. Too small, 5'2" at maturity, to sign up for the Infantry, he trained as a medical orderly before being shipped to Macedonia, where he was impressed not only by the suffering he witnessed but also by the consoling rhythms of daily life, even under the most trying circumstances. The second turning point was his relationship with Hilda Carline, herself a gifted artist and a member of a progressive circle in Hampstead, whom he married in 1925. With Hilda, Spencer discovered, and began to explore, his erotic self.

Yet, this is not a story of "happily ever after."

Spencer was attracted to other women—one of whom, Patricia Preece, became an obsession for him, though she was (by all accounts) lesbian. Hilda, distressed to the point of mental illness by Spencer's preoccupation with Patricia, divorced him. Spencer, in turn, married Patricia, though their marriage may have remained unconsummated. In any case, he remained attached to Hilda, whom he visited frequently and to whom he wrote passionate letters throughout his life—even after her death. He also had other love affairs, believing that all would be reconciled somehow, somewhere—if not on earth, then surely in heaven. At least in the heaven of his imagination.

It's this rather peculiar "heaven" that first captured my attention.

I think it's fair to say that Spencer was obsessed with the theme of the Resurrection—in varying situations and emotional contexts—throughout his life. One of the first of his paintings to be publicly exhibited was *John Donne Arriving in Heaven* (1911), implying, rather than portraying, Resurrection. Later, he focused on this subject explicitly in a series of intense paintings: *The Resurrection of the Good and the Bad* (1915), *The Resurrection, Cookham* (1924-26), *Resurrection* (1927), *The Resurrection of the Soldiers* (1927-28), *The Resurrection: Reunion* (1945), *Resurrection with the Raising of Jairus's Daughter* (1947), and *The Resurrection: Port Glasgow* (1947-50).

None of these paintings is orthodox in religious terms. Not only does Spencer choose ordinary people in ordinary situations climbing out of their graves, but he also portrays them as equally worthy of redemption. In Spencer's vision, there is no final selection process by which the "good" are separated from the "bad." Nor is there any depiction of the torments of the damned. Rather, everyone seems cheerfully restored to their flesh, happily contemplating the prospect of eternal life, as if it did not much differ from the pleasures they'd experienced on earth.

For Spencer, who considered the most mundane, even despised, aspects of human existence as full of illumination, heaven may truly have felt present to him on a daily basis. If so, it makes sense that he would try to give expression to this awareness in his painting.

For me, having grown up in the strict confines of 1950s American Catholicism—from which I later rebelled in predictable ways—such a vision was new and compelling. Not just in spiritual terms but also how I might view my complex, contradictory, seemingly fragmented, personal history. Perhaps there is another way, I thought, to view it whole?

The painting that most arrested me on first viewing is titled *The Dustman* or *The Lovers* (1934). In it, Spencer portrays the apotheosis of a single figure—that of the dustman, which translates into the American idiom as garbage collector. This figure, in the process of his transfiguration, is held up by a rather large female figure, understood to be his lover. Others, looking very much like Cookham villagers, regard his moment of personal transformation with awe. They hold the detritus of his trade up to him—wilted cabbages, teapots, and empty jam tins. For Spencer, what most of us would consider landfill was sacred. "I am on the side of angels," he once famously said, "and dirt."

Spencer labored his full adult life to integrate his natural sense of wonder—the belief his happy childhood instilled in him that heaven was all around him—with his mature understanding of sexual conflict, human destructiveness, and loss. In *The Dustman*, as in many of his Resurrection paintings, he manages to convince us—me at least—that such an integration is possible. These canvases are full of ordinary people and teeming life. Spencer's best vision was expansive, tolerant, and inclusive.

This is how I was beginning to view my own flawed, complex, seemingly disjointed, and fragmented history. From one perspective, it was a mess. No straight lines, no upward progress—but rather a series of awkward breaks, disruptions, failures, and transgressions. No order to speak of and certainly nothing to boast of. Yet, I was not able to exclude anything that mattered to me—even the most distressing or embarrassing of memories. To erase these details would feel like self-inflicted brainwashing. Like neuro-suicide.

So how did Spencer arrive at the capacity—in art at least—to imagine the random, seemingly unrelated bits of life, even the obviously discordant ones, as critical components of a larger design?

I can't answer this question on a psychological level, but surely the visual aspect of painting helped in its ability to convey an effect of simultaneity. Everything happening on the surface of a canvas is, after all, happening at the same time. Music and narrative art, in contrast, despite their recursive movements, unfold sequentially. While you may not exhaust an experience of a painting on a single viewing—certainly not if it is any good—you can still take it in visually. Spencer seems to have been particularly sensitive to this aspect of visual art. One of his deepest and most abiding influences was Trecento fresco painting, especially that of Giotto di Bondone.

Giotto's religious themes engaged him, given his own intensely religious imagination; yet, Giotto's gift for visual narrative may have appealed to Spencer even more. So taken was he with the cycle of frescoes that Giotto painted for his patron, Enrico Scrovegni, at a chapel constructed for this purpose in Padua (between 1303 and 1310) that he carried a small pocket edition of John Ruskin's commentary on it with him everywhere—even to war.

Spencer was clearly drawn to the idea of the Resurrection—where everything and everyone he'd ever loved would, he hoped or believed, be restored. But what was it about Giotto's vision, as displayed on the walls of the Scrovegni chapel, that so inspired him?

I wanted to know what Spencer knew—which he, in turn, attributed to Giotto. More particularly, I wanted to understand how memory, as shifty and malleable as it is, might possibly embrace one's ongoing history—with every quirk of detail, such as traumatic breaks, sudden and seemingly irrational shifts of direction, and the inevitable moments of shame and regret. Since Spencer took his inspiration from Giotto, this is where I went next.

I wasn't unfamiliar with Giotto's imagery—which I'd seen in print form. I'd even picked up two reproductions from the Scrovegni cycle at a garage sale in Minneapolis in the early 1970s. One of these portrays the crucifixion, with the cross in the center, cherubs with gold halos twisting their hands in a clear blue sky, and anguished mourners standing helplessly in attendance. The other shows the deposition from the cross, which also sets the drama of human passion against a serene and luminous background. I knew nothing about Giotto at the time but was drawn to something I saw in these prints. Was it the soft coloration—an effect of the way that paint is absorbed by fresh plaster? Or the way that Giotto had conveyed such intensity of emotion with effortless realism? I never framed or hung these prints, but I kept them, taking them out from time to time to gaze into the little world they depicted. Their reality was foreign to me, but it was one I wished to enter.

Many years later, I traveled with my second husband on our honeymoon to Assisi, where I viewed a full cycle of frescoes painted by Giotto in the Basilica of St. Francis. Once again, I was struck by the setting of precise human drama in lucid space. This sequence of paintings also created an experience of movement in time. Strolling past them, I could imagine the life of St. Francis passing before my eyes. The view was both prospective and retrospective. At any point, I could glimpse the future—or review the past—simply by turning my head. One frame led seamlessly to the next, giving the saint's life a feeling of tranquil inevitability. From birth, through conversion, to his life as a hermit and founder of a new monastic order, to death and assumption into heaven—each image was part of a single vision or destiny, though laid out sequentially like a hand of cards on a table.

I was enchanted. It was as if I could experience a life in individual moments, while also perceiving it whole. The fact that it was a saint's life—a kind of legend—didn't matter. Rather, it was the combination of visual and narrative art that appealed to me. Looked at one way, St. Francis's life unfolded as a series of events. Looked at another, it had the character of an epiphany.

When I encountered Stanley Spencer's Resurrection paintings, which seemed to me like attempts to hold all of life's contradictions in a single gaze, I could just begin to make sense of his fascination with Giotto. Like Giotto, Spencer aimed for a comprehensive vision, one that could embrace as much of life as he felt contained in himself. Such a vision, he believed—as I do now—was holy.

In May 2007, I have a chance to return to Italy. I travel with a friend who wants to research his maternal family lineage in the vicinity of Rome. I'm on a quest of my own: I want to go to Padua to view Giotto's frescoes in the Scrovegni Chapel.

In the meantime, I've acquired a hefty tome published in the Skira series of art books that details the restoration process of these frescoes while also showing close-ups of individual images and panels. But I need to experience this Chapel myself, perhaps as Spencer might have. Or wished he could.

The closest major city to Padua is Venice, so we fly there as a start. It's overcast, hot, and humid when we arrive at Marco Polo airport, where a transport service awaits us. This van takes us across a bridge to the floating city, where it deposits us at a parking lot. From this point, we must walk. Our Japanese woman assistant is distressed that we do not wish to leave our bags there to be transferred later. It's not that I distrust the service, but I want my clothes and cosmetics so I can take a shower as soon as possible at our hotel.

"There are three bridges," she says with a frown. We insist. As a result, my first experience of Venice is that of pulling my suitcase up and down several accordion pleats of steps. At last, we arrive at our hotel, which is not far from the train station. A definite plus.

At the hotel, there is a slight confusion about our reservation, which requires several rapid-fire exchanges in Italian between our patient assistant and the desk manager. These are followed by urgent cell phone calls from our assistant to the central travel agency she works for in London. At last, the problem is resolved, and we are ushered to our room—which is painted a vivid red—"bordello red" I think to myself—and adorned with gilded cherubs fixed to the walls on either side of the bed, which consists of twin mattresses pushed together and covered by a single blanket. My companion and I will struggle with the arrangement of the sheets (tucked under each mattress as if each were a single bed) and leave them in disarray every morning of our stay.

We shower, sleep, and then go out to explore this watery city. It's cooler, but still overcast, as we head toward the Jewish ghetto, which is a part of the Cannaregio district where we are staying. It's still early for the full tourist season, but the streets, lined with outdoor cafes, food vendors, and gelato stands, are full of strollers—some lugging suitcases, others idling, stopping to gaze into shop windows, or simply holding hands. We follow the crooked path before us, which crosses several small piazzas and more than one bridge before dipping down under a tunnel, called a *sottoporteggio*, into the ghetto.

Here there are fewer people, and I consider, with a chill, how it might have felt to be confined to this place—allowed to do business abroad by day but required to return by curfew and be locked in at night. This "ghetto"—a word that in its original meaning refers to its location in the New Foundry district of Venice, where armaments were once made—was established in 1516.

Shakespeare's *Merchant of Venice* springs to mind, along with the figure of Shylock, whose usury is uniformly condemned by the mercantile Venetians, who nonetheless depend on his wealth to finance their own ventures and who "out-merchant" him in the end. Ironically, my friend and I will observe a contemporary version of this crafty Venetian temperament, as vendors repeatedly attempt to short-change us—assuming that we do not understand European currency, are too affluent to care, or simply too preoccupied to notice.

By the end of the evening, we are lost. Whereas I have had the illusion that we were headed in the direction of the Piazza San Marco, it appears by our map that we are nowhere near it. Instead, we've been walking in circles, or spirals, through our own district—though somewhat north of the area of our hotel. Gradually, by sighting the train station, we make our way back. Over dinner on the awning-covered terrace at the Ristorante Roma, which borders the Grand Canal, we observe the sky darken over the water as lightning flashes in the distance and a torrent of rain falls.

The next day dawns beautifully clear. We locate the ample breakfast buffet and take our plates out into the garden, which consists of a small patio bordered by oleander bushes with pale pink and orange blossoms. A nameless songbird serenades us as we eat in the fresh, cool air.

Trains run every hour or so to Padua, which is, at most, a forty-minute ride away. We walk to the train station—the route now familiar, as we'd traced it the night before returning from the restaurant—and get our Eurail passes stamped. It's just short of 11:00 a.m. when we arrive.

Whereas Venice, even in the space of a few hours, has struck me as somewhat unreal—a mirage of a city rather than a place one might actually inhabit—Padua is clearly a working city, less alluring on the surface but more reassuringly business-like at heart. Here one will not find fanciful masks in shop windows nor mimes on street corners dressed in eighteenth-century costumes or pretending to be robots. Rather, people move with purpose—toward jobs, appointments, the mundane affairs of everyday life. We pass banks, corporate buildings, and department stores as we head down the main avenue toward the park that contains the Scrovegni Chapel. We arrive so quickly that it's hard to believe it is so close. We enter the inviting pathways of the park, realizing only belatedly that we've achieved our destination.

You must buy a timed ticket to view the Chapel, which admits a limited number of visitors every fifteen minutes. This schedule has been established by art conservators to control humidity in the Chapel—a prime factor in the deterioration of the frescoes.

We purchase our tickets and stroll through the adjoining archeological museum—a treasure in itself. Here we view a variety of Iron and Bronze Age artifacts, moving slowly forward in time. At last, I discover the excavation of a human form. It's a full-length skeleton of a man, lying atop the equally full-length skeleton of his horse. I am fascinated by this exhibit. Who was this man? And what kind of voyeur am I to consider the privacy of his bones?

At the airport in Minneapolis, I bought a book to read on my trip. My requirements were simple—something literary and not too bulky, as my bags were already full. I picked a paperback copy of Philip Roth's *Everyman*, though I'd not read Roth for years, considering him a bit too male-oriented for my taste. But *Everyman*—the title obviously referencing the medieval morality play—engrossed me.

Roth's tale begins with a death and memorial service for the protagonist, who narrates his life history over the course of the book—from his childhood in New Jersey, as the son of a Jewish father who ran a neighborhood jewelry store, through his adult career as an advertising executive, his three marriages, and his retirement to a community on the Jersey shore, where he devotes his time to painting, his first love.

There's nothing especially remarkable about this man's life—hence the title *Everyman*—yet he begins to seem exemplary. Not just of his own time, but of anyone's, male or female. He stumbles along; he does his best; he makes mistakes (which he cannot undo); achieves a modicum of personal, physical, and emotional satisfaction; reflects on his experience—and then dies.

Toward the end of the book, he visits his parents' graves in a neglected area of an even more neglected cemetery. There, he encounters an old-fashioned gravedigger, one who digs graves by hand—not unlike Shakespeare's gravedigger in *Hamlet*—who clues him in to the essentials of his craft. How it's best to use a common shovel, how it takes about a day to dig a six-foot-deep hole (square at the corners), how "it's got to be flat enough to lay a bed out on it," if it's done right—for the sake of the family and for the dead.

Roth's protagonist is comfortable in the company of this dignified elderly man, passing several hours with him as he works. His state of calm is all the more remarkable given his earlier excess of emotion at his parents' gravesite where he had broken down sobbing.

Here is the heart of Roth's novel—the hero's meditation

on death. It takes the form of a consideration of his parents' bodies or what's left of them—their bones.

> They were just bones, bones in a box, but their bones were his bones, and he stood as close to the bones as he could, as though the proximity might link him up with them and mitigate the isolation born of losing his future and reconnect him with all that had gone. . . . Between him and those bones there was a great deal going on, far more than now transpired between him and those still clad in their flesh. The flesh melts away but the bones endure. The bones were the only solace there was to one who put no stock in an afterlife and knew without a doubt that God was a fiction and this was the only life he'd have.

On the flight to Venice, I read about half of this short novel. Realizing how somber it was, I put it aside. I did not finish it until our return flight from Rome. By then, of course, I'd seen the skeleton of the unnamed warrior in the sarcophagus in the *museo archeologico*—and felt a tug from my own strict interior, the call of bone to bone.

Roth's hero concludes that "it was not going too far to say that his deepest pleasure now was at the cemetery. Here alone contentment was attainable." Yes, I thought when I read this. It's the satisfaction of knowing where it all ends—the arc of the narrative complete, with nowhere left to go.

But I did not think this thought until I was on my way home.

In the meantime, my companion and I wait outside the entrance to the Scrovegni Chapel, sitting on a low curb in the hot sun for fifteen minutes or so before we can be admitted to the cooled air of the antechamber—where we view a video about the exhibit. This interval allows for a literal breathing space after the exit of the previous group, which is necessary for the delicate temperature and humidity settings of the chapel. I am suddenly hyper-aware of the heat rising from my body, my faint underarm odor, beads of sweat on my skin. How carnal we are—in our heavy breath, our pads of muscle and flesh.

At last, we are admitted into a vaulted space—with full natural light flowing through windows placed high on one wall and recessed lights placed lower down, casting a discreet glow upwards. Having carefully perused my Skira book, I am familiar with the story, which narrates the drama of Christ's birth, death, and apotheosis. Alongside his is that of his mother Mary, beginning with her conception, growth into a young woman, and marriage to Joseph, leading to the birth of her son, her ordeal of grief at his crucifixion, and culminating in his resurrection and assumption into heaven. The chapel, evidently constructed as an act of expiation on the part of Reginaldo Scrovegni's son, Enrico, for his father's "sin" of usury, is also a visual hymn of praise to a woman of strength and courage.

The official name of this chapel is Santa Maria della Carita. Its dedication was March 25, 1305, the feast day of the Annunciation. And though God the Father sits enthroned at the apex of the chancel, it is Mary's story—in the figure of the angel Gabriel on the lower left and that of the Virgin on the right—that captures my interest.

There is plenty of suffering in her drama—as if Giotto understood the full range of human experience and emotion, delicately translating this knowledge into the media of paint and plaster and projecting it large—through the most powerful and resonant figures of his medieval imagination.

Still, the feeling quality of this space is light. Airy even. With its vaulted, azure ceiling, studded with brilliant gold stars, it reminds me of the chapel of Notre-Dame-de-Bon-Secours in Montreal. Newly restored, moreover, the images are fresh and clear. Giotto was the first to liberate his figures from rigid facial expressions and from a fixed gold background. As a result, his snapshot moments give the impression of movement—almost as if one were viewing freeze frames from Eadweard Muybridge's famous nineteenth-century photographs of a man (or a horse) running.

The dimensions of the chapel are compact. It was designed, after all, as a private place of worship for the Scrovegni family. Yet, their palazzo has long since vanished. Only the ruins of the Roman arena, purchased by Enrico Scrovegni along with the chapel he commissioned, remain. Two worlds juxtaposed— the classical and pre-modern—themselves underpinned by even more ancient cultures and bones.

At last I turn to face the entrance wall, the one that depicts the drama of the Last Judgment. Prepared to resist the finality of this vision—the absolute separation of good from evil, right from wrong—I am struck instead by an odd visual effect. Christ, seated in the center of a jagged (almost psychedelic) rainbow of light, seems less triumphant to me than wounded, bleeding from one side. To his left, his halo turns crimson, as if, like a balloon, it has developed a leak—or is hemorrhaging. All down this side, naked forms fall, borne off by demons to endless torment. To Christ's right, the redeemed assemble, fully clothed.

The iconography is traditional, yet I can't shake the feeling that Giotto has presented us with a challenge. It's the bleeding hole in Christ's halo that complicates the picture. If the so-called damned are a manifestation of his wound, how are we to maintain the distinction between those who are saved and those who are not? Both share the same visual field.

Spencer's *The Dustman*, I believe, owes much to Giotto's vision of life held suspended in a clear meditative gaze. As if one could contemplate one's own destiny—from beginning to end—as part of an unbroken arc of shining color. Everything included, nothing left out. All one's pleasures and errors detailed, acknowledged, dramatized, revealed.

Of *The Dustman*, Spencer said, "it is like watching and experiencing the inside of a sexual experience. They are all in a state of anticipation and gratitude to each other."

On returning from Padua, my friend and I violate the order of our beds—so closely connected, though also so strictly sheeted. We touch each other in every private place, mingling body parts as if they were interchangeable. Then we hold each other for a long time afterwards.

Grateful.

Down the Mississippi

Down the Mississippi

Down the Miss-iss-ippi
Down the muddy Miss-iss-ippi
Where the boats go pu-ush. . . .
  —Skipping rope rhyme

I live in Minneapolis on the east bank of the Mississippi River, which begins in northern Minnesota as a stream so small you can walk across it on stepping stones and flows all the way to the Gulf of Mexico.

Although I grew up in St. Louis, also on the Mississippi, I didn't really know where Minneapolis was, until I looked at a map. So much for my grade-school geography lessons. I'd been living and teaching at a small liberal arts college in Vermont and needed a new job. The University of Minnesota, an enormous urban campus divided by the Mississippi River, offered me one, so I moved in 1971 to a neighborhood called Prospect Park, where I have lived ever since. It interested me that I was returning to the Midwest—just upriver from where I'd grown up. Was this an accident of fate? Or was there some hidden meaning in this move?

Was something calling me back?

I'm a restless person and move around a lot. In my second (commuting) marriage I spent at least half of the year in Oakland, California, not far from the San Francisco Bay and the vast and beautiful Pacific Ocean. I loved making trips to the beach, watching the big waves crash against the shore. When I returned to Minneapolis after the end of that marriage, I began to travel more frequently—at least once a month and sometimes more often—to attend professional meetings, visit with my daughter living in New York, or return to St. Louis to see my mother in the neighborhood where I'd grown up. I was away from Minneapolis, it seemed, as much as I was home.

Yet, I was always aware of the river, less than a mile from my house, which I would drive across to get almost anywhere I was going in the course of my day and where I walked along the parkway close to the water. These were slow, dreamy walks, no matter what the season, and I'd invariably stop for a time to sit under a tree or on a rock and gaze at the water.

The Mississippi River has been my silent companion through the early and middle years of my life.

After my dad died, I had a fantasy that his body, which was not found for two days, had floated all the way down the river into the Gulf. Because I never saw him after the moment of his disappearance and was not allowed to attend his funeral, I had no real sense of where he'd gone. It seemed as likely as not that he'd been swept by the river to its own headlong destination.

Of course, I know better. I've been to his gravesite, seen the granite marker, and know where he lies. Yet, I can never quite put aside my childhood thought. So the river feels familiar to me—and comforting. As if that is the place where my life has continuity and meaning.

Toward the end of 2008, after Christmas, I travel to New Orleans with a friend. I don't think about this too much ahead of time, as I'm just too busy. My brother Ron died suddenly the preceding summer. Traveling to St. Louis for his memorial service, followed by the first effort with my brother Bob to begin clearing out Ron's house, has pretty much exhausted me. In many ways, I am glad to deal with the more mundane and predictable routines of university life over the course of fall semester. But I'm also aware that New Orleans is the city where one branch of my mother's New World ancestry took root.

The first fur-trading settlers of St. Louis are among my French forbears who traveled up the Mississippi to the site they established on the west bank of the river to further their trade with the local, mostly Osage, Indian tribes. You might say that New Orleans is one of the places where my family history, at least on record, begins. It's also just northwest of the place where the Great River Road literally ends.

The road I had driven from Minneapolis to St. Louis, marked by the sign of a paddleboat wheel, follows the Mississippi river all the way to the Gulf of Mexico. It doesn't even end in New Orleans but at the tip of a long finger of land that extends away from the coast until it melts into the water. Though I'd visited New Orleans in the past, I'd never thought of exploring this road. It would be a shame to miss this opportunity now.

On a raw, overcast day, my friend and I rent a car and begin our quest. At first, we get lost trying to locate Belle Chasse, the town south of New Orleans where we can connect with the Great River Road, which is marked by a trail of green dots on our map. Once we make the proper turn-off, we find ourselves on a rather nondescript road bordered by a chain of restaurants, gas stations, and strip malls—not at all what I had imagined. I'd pictured a brighter, warmer day, for starters, being so far south. But it's cold enough that we keep the heater on and the windows rolled up for the entire trip. Also, there's nothing I would consider "scenic" about this route. We could be on any remote highway anywhere in the country, so dull and repetitive is the landscape. Once we've begun, however, I want to go on.

We pass through a series of small towns with names like Wills Point, Phoenix, Pointe a la Hache, Bohemia, Happy Jack, Port Sulphur, Tropical Bend, and Triumph. There is plenty of oncoming traffic, though fewer signs of habitation, as we drive farther south. The light is beginning to wane, and now also we are driving into mist. A light fog obscures the road ahead, making it even harder to distinguish between one town and another. It's suddenly as if we've gone off road, beyond anything that feels ordinary or familiar. Houses and other evidence of human activity decrease as we continue. The land on either side of the road seems thinner, less substantial. We pass the last town marked on my map: Venice.

We come to a white sign with red and blue lettering that reads:

WELCOME
YOU HAVE REACHED THE SOUTHERNMOST
POINT IN LOUISIANA
GATEWAY TO THE GULF

A mile or two beyond, we come to another sign that says Road Closed. We drive around it, as the gravelly dirt road seems passable. It is now hard to see more than a few feet ahead or on either side of the car. But we can discern a canal on the right, and a series of fishermen, widely spaced from one another, silently fishing the water. Some have parked their trucks nearby, while others appear to have materialized out of the mist. Despite the gathering darkness, no one seems in a hurry to depart. Rather, they seem like features of the landscape, risen from the fog and water.

We ourselves seem like immaterial spirits—as no one takes notice of us, much less our disregard of the Road Closed sign. Perhaps there is a fellowship of travelers that is beyond prohibition.

We drive as far as we can go. Until the road stops and there is nothing but water ahead. We get out of the car and walk a few steps further. Water on both sides now, merging into a larger body of water softly shrouded in darkness. The spit of land we stand on is hardly more substantial than what lies before us. A thickening, you might say, of darkness—composed of mist, a handful of dirt, and silence.

Acknowledgements

These chapters have appeared in various forms in the following publications:

"Great River Road" in *Fugue*, no. 26 (Winter 2003-04), pp. 73-90. "When Other Worlds Invite Us" in *The Laurel Review*, v. 44, no 2 (Fall 2010), pp. 42-55.

છ૪

Great River Road began in my imagination at my daughter's wedding but took shape slowly over time. The people who have contributed to its unfolding feel like extended family.

The first friends who supported this project are the wonderful women who invited me to live in their Berkeley homes (sometimes for as much as a month at a time) while they were away: Carol Cosman, Tina Gillis, Gayle Greene, Claire Kahane, Victoria Nelson, and Brenda Webster. Their beautiful houses were like private writing retreats, where I had the space of reflection I needed to compose the early chapters of the book.

I also want to thank the women who participated (at various times) in my East Bay writing group: Janet Adelman, Marilyn Fabe, Gayle Greene, Claire Kahane, Mardi Louisell, and Wendy Martin. I am grateful to them all for their sensitive and probing responses. In addition, the Bay Area Psychobiography Group (some of whom are named above) read and commented on several essays in progress. Their insights startled me into new ways of thinking. I am especially grateful to Ramsay Breslin, not only for her gracious hosting but also for her searching questions and perceptions. Stephen Walrod, one of the founders of this group, said something about one of the chapters that altered its shape while also giving me cause for personal reflection. David Allswang offered not only the comfort of his aerie apartment in north Berkeley at a critical stage of the book's development, but also his belief in me as a writer.

I took long walks—so critical for my writing proces—with many of the above in which we talked about our lives. There is no way to express how meaningful these (now lost) conversations were, nor how they continue to resonate in me.

In Minnesota, I have also been fortunate in my long-term and more recent friendships. My closest friends from the University of Minnesota, Shirley Garner and Toni McNaron, have always believed in me and my eclectic path in life. They have stood by me no matter what, especially through the phase of transition I describe in the first chapters of this book.

The University of Minnesota has offered its support through the grants and leaves that I have enjoyed over the years it took to complete this project, as well as its appointment of me as Regents Professor, an honor that has provided many additional resources, especially in the forms of travel and research. Nasir Sakandar, my research assistant for the past three years, deserves special recognition for his support of both my scholarly and creative writing endeavors.

My long-term association with the New Directions Program in Washington DC, has given me courage to pursue my most pressing writing aims. Locally, the Interdisciplinary Studies in Psychoanalysis Group, a subsidiary of the Minnesota Psychoanalytic Institute and Society, has provided valuable feedback on my work-in-progress. This society, as well as the local chapter of the American Association for Psychoanalysis in Clinical Social Work, the Society for Psychoanalytic Studies, and the Minnesota Jung Association, has been very receptive to my writing.

At a critical moment in time, Marly Rusoff, a founding member and sponsor of The Loft Literary Center, suggested that I articulate more clearly the connection between the Mississippi River and the subjects of memoir and memory. To her thoughtful reading, I owe the last chapter of this book.

To my extended family—including my former in-laws and especially my ex-mother-in-law, Nellie May Gohlke—I owe the understanding of how a complex family system can sustain its members through difficulty, pain, and loss. They have shown their love for me by accepting me as I am. My daughter, Jessica Gohlke, is everything I have ever wished for in a daughter. She is at the center of everything that is good in my life.

More recent friends have also helped this book to come into being. I am lucky to have found a superb writing group in the Twin Cities, whose members have responded to my writing with thoughtful criticism and enthusiasm. I'm especially appreciative of the reading and comments of Elise Sanders on the (more or less) completed manuscript. In addition, Angella Kassube, who produced a wonderful motion poem for my prose poem, "The Angel of Duluth," and has produced an equally wonderful book trailer for *Great River Road*.

Two people deserve special recognition—Ilse Jawetz, my San Francisco psychotherapist, who helped me through a major disruption of my life, and Michael Young, whom I met when I was part of the way through this project. Ilse, a senior training analyst at the San Francisco Psychoanalytic Institute, helped guide me through the disruption of my second marriage into the next phase of life. She died in 2012, but I think of her often and her realistically sage advice. Michael, to whom this book is dedicated, is in many ways like Ilse—accepting of my complex history and urging me toward the person I want to become. Much of the chapter "Bountiful" was composed in his house on the prairie. He also accompanied me to the end of the Great River Road. Together, we imagine our lives into the future.

identify

1. P. 14 -
Trouble reading
Maps - Written
directions

2. failed 1st
driving test

3. Stick Shift

Author Bio

Madelon Sprengnether is a poet, memoirist, and literary critic. She is Regents Professor of English at the University of Minnesota, where she teaches poetry, theory, and creative nonfiction. She is a graduate of the New Directions Program in Psychoanalytic Thinking in Washington, DC, and she is a member of numerous regional and national psychoanalytic organizations, including the Minnesota Psychoanalytic Society and Institute, the American Psychoanalytic Association, and Division 39 of the American Psychological Association.

Sprengnether is the author of two books of poetry, *The Normal Heart* and *The Angel of Duluth*; two memoirs, *Rivers, Stories, Houses, Dreams* and *Crying at the Movies*; and a co-edited collection of travel essays by women, *The House on Via Gombito*; in addition to numerous works of feminist psychoanalytic criticism.

For more information, visit her author website: www.madelonsprengnether.com

About New Rivers Press

New Rivers Press emerged from a drafty Massachusetts barn in winter 1968. Intent on publishing work by new and emerging poets, founder C. W. "Bill" Truesdale labored for weeks over an old Chandler & Price letterpress to publish three hundred fifty copies of Margaret Randall's collection, *So Many Rooms Has a House But One Roof.*

Nearly four hundred titles later, New Rivers, a non-profit and now teaching press based since 2001 at Minnesota State University Moorhead, has remained true to Bill's goal of publishing the best new literature—poetry and prose—from new, emerging, and established writers.

New Rivers Press authors range in age from twenty to eighty-nine. They include a silversmith, a carpenter, a geneticist, a monk, a tree-trimmer, and a rock musician. They hail from cities such as Christchurch, Honolulu, New Orleans, New York City, Northfield (Minnesota), and Prague.

Charles Baxter, one of the first authors with New Rivers, calls the press "the hidden backbone of the American literary tradition." Continuing this tradition, in 1981 New Rivers began to sponsor the Minnesota Voices Project (now called Many Voices Project) competition. It is one of the oldest literary competitions in the United States, bringing recognition and attention to emerging writers. Other New Rivers publications include the American Fiction Series, the American Poetry Series, New Rivers Abroad, and the Electronic Book Series.

Please visit our website newriverspress.com for more information.